Ingrained
LEGACY

Ingrained
LEGACY

Saskatchewan

Pioneer

Woodworkers

1870-1930

JUDITH SILVERTHORNE

SPIRAL COMMUNICATIONS INC.

Photographs of all woodwork pieces by Linda McDowell.
Scanning of woodwork photographs by Aaron Silverthorne.

Copy-edited by Karen Steadman.
Cover photographs by Linda McDowell.
Cover and book design by Duncan Campbell.
Printed and bound in Canada at Gauvin Press.

National Library of Canada Cataloguing in Publication Data

Silverthorne, Judith, 1953-
Ingrained legacy: Saskatchewan pioneer woodworkers, 1870-1930 /
Judith Silverthorne.

Includes bibliographical references.
ISBN 0-9732879-0-X

1. Woodworkers—Saskatchewan—Biography. 2. Woodwork—
Saskatchewan—History. I. Title.

NK9697.S54 2003   684'.08'09227124   C2003-905599-X

Spiral Communications Inc.
Regina, Saskatchewan, Canada

The Canada Council for the Arts
Le Conseil des Arts du Canada

*This book is dedicated to all the people who immigrated to Saskatchewan
and their offspring, especially to the woodworkers,
who gave so much of themselves to enrich this province.*

In particular, I dedicate this book to my grandparents:

*Adolf & Elizabeth (Krahenbil) Assman
&
Henry & Mary (Vipond) Iles.*

*May the memories of all our ancestors live in our hearts
and continue to be part of our heritage.*

contents

PREFACE—i

INTRODUCTION—1
In the Beginning
Research Criteria
Carpenters & Woodworkers
Training & Experience
Locations
Environment & Materials
Tools & Shops
Artifacts
Styles
Women's Roles
Family Participation
Ethnic Groups
First Nations
Summation

MAJOR WOODWORKERS

INDIVIDUAL WOODWORKERS—95

ETHNIC GROUPS

APPENDICES

BIBLIOGRAPHY—165

Acknowledgements

My heartfelt thank you and deep appreciation go to the Saskatchewan Heritage Foundation for the significant financial support and endorsement they have provided to make this project possible. I especially thank Garth Pugh & Frank Korvemaker for their invaluable insights and assistance. Thank you also to the Saskatchewan History and Folklore Society for their important funding, and to the Canada Council, Jean A. Chalmers Fund for the Craft.

My gratitude to Linda McDowell, a wonderful travelling companion, and for her excellent photography, which has made these woodworkers come alive and this project a pleasure to work on.

Thanks also to the numerous community newspapers around the province, as well as the many community museums, especially those in Broadview, Duck Lake, Esterhazy, Meadow Lake, Moosomin, Rocanville, Prince Albert, Prud'homme, Verigin, and Whitewood, and the Western Development Museums at Saskatoon and Yorkton, and the staff at Batoche National Historic Park.

Thanks to the Saskatchewan Archives Board, and the collectors, both private and commercial, who so willingly shared their knowledge and allowed photographs to be taken of their artifacts, especially Lindsay Anderson, Doug Bentham, Ruth Bittner, George Chopping, Ralph Jarotski, Pete Mandziak, John McGowan, Pearl Jamieson, Mac Provich, and Susan Whitney. Thank you John Kort, BSA, MSC (Shelterbelt Biologist/ Agroforester with PFRA).

My thanks also to all the people who allowed me to explore the woodworking worlds of their loved ones.

J

PREFACE

I CONDUCTED THE RESEARCH FOR THIS PROJECT OVER A THREE-YEAR period from 1992-1995. Throughout the spring, summer and fall of each of these years, Linda McDowell and myself travelled all over Saskatchewan in search of woodworkers, who immigrated and lived in the province between 1870 and 1930. Linda McDowell captured the majority of the photographs, concentrating on the woodwork artifacts, while I did the black and white copy work of the individuals' portraits and early environment, and interviewed family members.

We scoured cemeteries, town offices, rural churches, local community members, friends and family members of the woodworkers, museums, galleries, and collectors. We investigated storage places, garages, basements, attics, barns, granaries, and backyards. We hiked cross-country, checked out abandoned and dilapidated buildings in fields, and traversed many back roads and little used highways to a multitude of farms, cities, and towns. We travelled hundreds of miles, contacted dozens of people, and set up photography equipment for over 1200 slides and photographs.

Throughout the course of our explorations, we encountered many wonderful people and made many new friends, acquaintances, and contacts. We also delighted in extraordinary finds and treasures, the majority of which had been hidden away for many years, and we enjoyed the fascination and pride of the family members as they led us to amazing discoveries. Our early pioneer woodworkers were truly gifted, ingenious, and creative.

All of the original research material can be found in the Saskatchewan Archives Board in Regina, and the Saskatchewan Heritage Foundation holds copies of the final summation report.

INTRODUCTION

THE PURSUIT OF DREAMS AND A SEARCH FOR A BETTER life has been a driving force in motivating humankind to relocate over the ages, and the massive waves of settlers who immigrated to the Canadian prairies around the turn of the twentieth century were no exception. Millions came on the quest, bringing with them a diversity of backgrounds and skills, seeking previously unheard of opportunities. None were more welcomed or valued than the carpenters, woodworkers and furniture makers who ventured forth on high expectations.

For the most part these talented craftspeople were not disappointed by the outcome, although uncertainties abounded and their anticipations differed considerably from actual realizations. The change in stature from their homelands, their varied ethnicity and religious backgrounds, the extent of their training, the diversity of the lands where they settled, and the availability of materials and tools, had a bearing on the method and degree of success in their chosen livelihoods.[1]

Today the quality of remaining buildings, pieces of furniture, and works of art still located around Saskatchewan give an indication of the large number of skilled carpenters and woodworkers who enriched and formed the basis of the province—the majority of which appeared on the scene between 1870 and 1930. However, a smattering of these resourceful craftspeople arrived a few decades earlier, and settled in places that were actually extensions of previously established outposts and forts such as Fort Carleton and Cumberland House.[2]

IN THE BEGINNING

Although European influence began on the prairies as early as the 1690s with the onset of fur trading ventures and explorations by Henry Kelsey, and later by others such as Sieur de la Vérendrye in 1737,[3] Peter Pond in 1778, and Philip Turnor in 1779,[4] the initial more permanent settlements in pre-Saskatchewan (with the exception of trading posts and forts) date from the 1860s. The establishment of one of the earliest permanent communities is credited to Reverend James Nisbet[5] at Prince Albert, where he founded a Presbyterian Mission along the banks of the North Saskatchewan River in 1866. This later developed into an agricultural district with the aid of Nisbet, the nearby William Miller family of what became known as Miller's Hill,[6] the McDonalds, and other perseverant settlers, several of whom also demonstrated their talents with wood.

Subsequent homesteaders continued to situate themselves in the Prince Albert area, and along the Churchill and Saskatchewan Rivers until the 1870s.[7] At this time, due to government influences,[8] homesteading began moving south towards Battleford and eastward into the Carrot River valley.[9] A short time later colonization followed a general township pattern across the prairie when settlement increased in the 1880s with the introduction of the railway and other improved transportation routes. The most massive influx occurred in a systematic and orderly fashion in the 1890s, and climaxed during the decade starting in 1896.[10] By the end of the first decade after the turn of the century the population had increased an overwhelming five times to over one million people.[11]

Small shelf unit made by an unknown woodworker

Harvesting with horses

Political persecution, religious suppression, economic hardships, over-population, rigid class distinctions, and other oppressive conditions forced many people from Eastern Europe to become immigrants. Others came from Western Europe and the United States, but not all of them arrived from countries abroad or south of the border. Some appeared from within Canada, mostly from the more heavily-populated eastern provinces of Ontario and Quebec.

At the time the pioneers began venturing in earnest into what was eventually to become Saskatchewan the land was virtually untouched, offering opportunities often filled with unsuspected hardships. Travel by rail was available only as far as Brandon, Manitoba by 1882, and from there they had to travel across the wind-swept plains by oxen and carts or covered wagons with only a few well-chosen essential belongings.

As the settlers eked out homesteads and cleared land, a need quickly developed for carpenters to construct necessary buildings. There seems to have been an abundance of these skilled craftspeople, who either lived in a particular community or were willing to travel fair distances to work. Assembling a rudimentary one-room shack in a single day became only a matter of course,[12] and soon homesteaders' shanties dotted the prairie landscape like tiger lilies in June. Communities developed just as quickly with pockets of immigrants from the same original homelands gathered together, often with family members nearby.

While the immigrants brought what belongings they could, this often meant a small token of what they actually required. Many other articles they needed for furnishing their homes were only available from abroad or from Eastern manufacturers at high premiums with major shipping problems and costs attached. The manufacturers were not interested in establishing branch retail businesses or factories in the west. They only wanted to ship the finished product, eventually supplying mail order catalogues, which augmented their philosophies. Local businesses for purchasing household articles were practically non-existent for many of the early years.

RESEARCH CRITERIA

For the most part, the criteria for the research has been one of dates that include early colonization in Saskatchewan between 1870 and 1930, and reflect those who did the majority of their work during that interval. Most importantly, the craftspeople included were those who worked with hand tools, many of which they made for themselves.

In addition, before 1870 there was little demand for the craft. After 1930 and the Second World War, local stores and mail-order catalogues provided easier access and were more economically feasible for most household requirements. This caused the demand for the services of many of the previous woodworkers to dwindle. As well, the work of the craftsmen began reflecting the more commercial styles available through eastern catalogues and bigger local centres, usually at the request of their clientele.

The majority of the information contained within this book comes from a personal survey, which I implemented through correspondence, and while travelling across a substantial amount of Saskatchewan with professional photographer, Linda McDowell, conducting personal interviews and photographing slides of the numerous artifacts.

Although this research does not prove conclusive, a great effort has gone into trying to obtain as much information as possible from various sources by contacting private, government, and local community museums and archives, requesting information over radio and through daily and weekly newspapers, as well as communicating with as many family, friends, and former neighbours of the craftspeople as possible. Also the elderly in various communities, and the personnel in local town offices and businesses, proved very helpful in directing the search, as did private and commercial collectors and other knowledgeable people in the field. Local history books were not consulted extensively, however many of them were searched for known names, and follow-ups were conducted of other craftspeople found in them during these searches.

A large number of these craftspeople were unidentified until recently, except perhaps for a select few who were recognized by individual collectors or held in esteem by family members. Occasionally, a woodworker and his artifacts were kept in high regard over the years in some communities, but by-and-large the younger generations seem unaware of the resources left behind by their predecessors.

Various speaker's chairs in Saskatchewan legislative building, attributed to John McGuirl of Moosomin

In many cases the names of the expert craftspeople now known were difficult to ascertain, and sometimes little information was available about them. At times there was merely a hint of a last name and a vague idea of where the person lived. At other times there was only a solitary piece of exquisite furniture, its maker nameless, its origins unknown. Sadly, there are those who will never be identified and some details of certain craftspeople's lives and work, may have been lost forever.

On the positive side, most areas of the province seem to have had artisans to call their own. Although some have already been mentioned, others of significance stand out. In the Canora district, John Danchilla may be remembered for his furniture making and fretwork, while Ralph Samuels, who built many homes, churches and barns in the same area, supplemented his income with furniture building. A little farther northeast at Whitebeech, William Krochak was prolific in church artifacts, and towards the west at Hazel Dell, John Wilson intricately carved the likes of church fonts and grandfather clocks.

Names like Jacob Armbruster, John Fessor, and Jacob Wendel are important in the Neudorf region for wardrobes and other household pieces of merit, while Vacla Yecny is known at Esterhazy for his superb china cabinets. George and Jack Parley helped build much of the town of Grenfell, besides pieces of furniture and the first private steam-powered boat in the district. Near Krydor and Hafford, John Hazlebower was a prolific builder of small items for churches.

Cradle built by a member of the Timm family of Neudorf

Nels Swenson produced fine tables, chairs and cupboards at Broadview, but his life was short and not many of his pieces remain. Nearby in Whitewood William(?) Stevens[on][13] worked as a professional chip carver, while Fred Daniels made rocking chairs and footstools. Other neighbours in the area like Oscar Salo, excelled in birchbark containers with interlocking joints, and John Howard produced violins and carved bishop's chairs.

Malcolm McDonald of Southey was an exceptionally creative man with talents in wood, stone and painting. Meanwhile, to the south in the tree-barren regions at Coderre, Charles Smith created functional items from used apple and cheese boxes. In the Gravelbourg area the names of Ferdinand Gauthier, Mr. (?) Tousignan, and Joseph Kleisinger are familiar for a variety of wood artifacts from carvings to furniture. During the same time at Maple Creek, Melvin Zeigler fashioned chairs from buffalo horns, and George Hammond and Ted Perrin made cabinets, counters and display cases for stores and bars.

Near Battram, Knut Leverson excelled at musical instruments, particularly the crafting of violins. Anton Soehn at Fox Valley was a woodworker of note, as was Adolf Steinke of Kelstern. Farther north at Prud'homme, Lorenzo Paquin fashioned violins and rocking chairs, while Sam Kripki from Cudworth built cupboards, and at St. Denis, Adelard Moyen worked as a carpenter and furniture builder.

James McGuirl from Moosomin was known around the province before 1912 for his remarkable interior work on churches and Masonic lodges, as well as for desks, chairs and other furniture that sat in Government House and the Legislative Building. He actually operated a full-fledged furniture factory, and also supplied hockey sticks for the west.

Nearby at Kenosee, Samuel Rogers operated a sawmill business, building bookcases and library desks, and David Cunningham in the Kipling region built game tables among other items.

Philip Turner, of the fur-trading generation, worked in the Coxby area in the early- to mid-1800s. A couple of decades later, about 1866, near Prince Albert, Rev. James Nisbet, George Pease, Arnold Russell, and a fellow by the last name of MacDonald, made a wide variety of household artifacts.

Shupe chair, carved with an ax

L.E. Shupe will be remembered for crafting a chair, which was hewn from green timber. The only tools he used were an axe, a saw, a brace and bit, and a hammer. He made it on the east bank of the North Saskatchewan River, six miles down stream from Fort Carlton. Although constructed in November 1944, refinished in 1972, and is not within the general scope of this book, it is a fine example of workmanship with crude tools.

Farther west and south at Maymont, Harold Coombs became renowned for making unusual figurines and ornaments that he displayed in the grass and trees about his farmyard, while Edward Wilmot built cabinets and did beautiful carvings in the local Anglican church.

In another corner of the province at Loon Lake, a little later than the focus of this book but still worth mention, the Loon Lake Toy Factory was in operation in the early 1940s. Four ambitious Sudaten German farmers

Lunch time at harvest

Ploughing with oxen

launched it: Franz Rehwald, Heinrich Palme, Anton Hocher and Emil Hecht. Others also helped, but the community enterprise, although off to a good start in 1939, only lasted for a couple of years. Problems with drying wood, exporting their products and salesmanship were the culprits to its demise.

In that same general vicinity at Meadow Lake, Bart Armstrong made necessary household furnishings for his own homestead, and near Rapid View, Aaron Weins made willow armchairs, walking canes and china cabinets. Many other woodworkers of note were scattered around the province, and some areas seem to have abundant numbers, but there are those where none have become evident. This may have been due in part to the fact that there was a distinct lack of available materials in some areas, such as the grasslands situated in the south and the sandhills of the west central region of the province.

Southeast Saskatchewan around Estevan and Weyburn is another of those void districts. In fact, in the spring of 1874, the North West Mounted Police stopped along Long Creek, two miles from the American border, and there established Woodend Post, appropriately named because of the obvious sudden lack of wood or trees in the vicinity.[14] Thus it is not unexpected at this point in time that woodworkers of note will come to light in that area.

CARPENTERS AND WOODWORKERS

Although those who were strictly carpenters and builders were vitally important to early settlement and community life, providing houses, barns, businesses, churches, schools and other social gathering places and buildings, actually locating and naming all the carpenters was an undertaking beyond the scope of this project. Instead, the focus of this book is on those people who contributed to the craft of working with wood on a personal or smaller scale than that of larger structures. Yet, many of the woodworkers that have been included in this study were also carpenters of some sort or another, or at times did this type of "rough" work to supplement their incomes.

In fact, many of the woodworkers augmented their earnings at intervals throughout their careers. The majority of them originally applied for homesteads, and the requirements for proving[15] these kept the craftspeople occupied much of the time. Whenever the opportunity arose, they worked away from their farms, toiling as hired hands, helping with harvest, and at whatever odd jobs they could find.

If they lived along a rail line as many such as Olaf Pearson of the Percival area did, they kept the miles of track clear of snow in the winter and in good repair year round.[16] There were those nomadic types like William Zaderogzny from the Alvena/Cudworth area and John Kadyba of the Krydor/Blaine Lake district, who travelled about the countryside during the summer months, building churches and working on larger projects. In the winter they made beds and other household furniture in exchange for room and board.

Some enterprising craftspeople, John McGuirl at Moosomin being one, eventually left their farms and established successful businesses within nearby towns. There were others like Joachim Pilon of Melville, who launched extensive commercial ventures in the towns immediately upon their arrival. However, only a handful did their work on a business- or factory-type scale. Mostly the woodworkers did small amounts each year for themselves and perhaps for a few local people, and often the work was done during the quieter winter months when other occupations were scarce.[17]

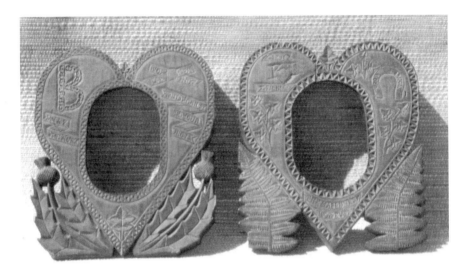

Heart-shaped frames by Taylor of the Broadview area

TRAINING AND EXPERIENCE

Differences in style may be attributed to the methods in which wood-working was learned in each area of Europe and other countries from which most of the immigrants stemmed. Although some of the wood-workers were obviously self-taught, or learned as apprentices, there were opportunities for more formal education and training in many of the woodworking fields in several countries. For instance, in England there was a distinction in the trades such as carpenters, joiners, cabinetmakers, and other woodworkers like woodsmen, sawyers, coach makers, coopers, turn-ers, pattern makers, wheelwrights, shipwrights, wainwrights, and whit-tlers.[18] Carvers were also highly skilled and received extensive education.

Some of the English woodworkers who immigrated to Saskatchewan in the early years had obtained considerable training or had their "papers," like William(?) Stevens[on] from Whitewood probably did, but a significant number did not.[19] Although many guilds of the various artisans existed in some form or another, the organization of these specialized crafts eventu-ally broke down when they were transported to the Canadian Prairies.

Transplanting European society simply didn't work when it came to facing the conditions and necessities of the new unbroken land. The

George Parley Homestead, ca. 1885

trained and educated woodworkers seldom remained specialists nor continued exactly what they were most proficient at. For instance, those who might be skilled as carvers quickly found building rudimentary furniture for immediate use was more prudent. Sheer necessity to produce other items and to do what was needed to earn a living prevailed instead.[20]

Common sense ensued for most certified woodworkers. Although there were those like Pearson, who painstakingly decorated everything he made, whether it was a simple practical box to hold drill bits or a more substantial desk or cabinet, there simply wasn't a need, nor sufficient demand for specialized woodworkers to pursue their own discipline.

Because the population was so wide spread across the province, guilds were neither formed nor practical to form in their new land. Even the concept of apprenticeship was not a considered form of teaching in the way it had been in their homelands. Although the reason has not been totally determined, there was no mention of apprentices in any of the

cases of the woodworkers researched. They were a solitary bunch, often isolated from other craftsmen of their kind.

There were influences of a sort in some cases affecting the designs of the Saskatchewan craftsperson. For instance, a woodworker of one culture might try to replicate a pattern or "borrow" an idea or style from another, particularly for added features. Otherwise, woodworkers only had their own experience and knowledge to rely upon for designs. In later years, they were undoubtedly influenced by the examples found in mail-order catalogues from eastern factories and stores, but for the most part they used their own resources or derived inspiration from their surroundings.

LOCATIONS

Not surprisingly, the most plentiful number of woodworkers lived along the treeline that cuts diagonally across the province. Others resided in the communities that grew beside the railway lines: one group because their workable commodities were close at hand, and the other because lumber and goods could be shipped easily out to them, although at a price.[21] There were other pockets of woodworkers in various treed areas of Saskatchewan, and even those who persevered where there were no trees, such as the case with Charles Smith of Coderre, who manufactured furniture from recycled products.

ENVIRONMENT AND MATERIALS

Their environments influenced their work habits to a vast degree, and this was undoubtedly a major deciding factor for the types of products they chose to make. Secluded from larger centres, fellow woodworkers, a lack of common materials, and other resources and information, the craftsmen plodded along on their own ingenuity. The immigrants found the nature of the prairies harsh and unforgiving, as they struggled to maintain a livelihood in their chosen field. Long, cold winters, short, hot summers, unfamiliarity, and lonely and solitary conditions prevailed to such an extent that they were forced into self-sufficiency.

Made by an unknown furniture maker, possibly from the Canora area

The availability of materials, both local and imported, also played a significant part in determining the types of products manufactured. According to John Kort of the Prairie Farm Rehabilitation Administration with Agriculture Canada,[22] there were several types of hardwood trees readily available in Saskatchewan for woodworkers around the turn of the century. The main species were birch, aspen poplar, green ash, and Manitoba maple. Softwoods like jackpine and white spruce were abundant in the northern areas. Pine and spruce were preferred for construction because they were easy to cut and durable. Tamarack, a minor species, was not used much. There was plenty of poplar, the trembling aspen variety found commonly throughout the province, which many woodworkers probably used for basic furniture.[23] A soft hardwood, it's very light and easy to cut.

American elm, the hardest wood next to oak, grew predominantly in the river valleys of eastern Saskatchewan.[24] Green ash on the other hand, was available all over the prairies, although the larger trees were found in the forest fringes, with the biggest at Cumberland House. However, green ash tends to crack a little, and limited amounts of furniture making were done with it. Mountain ash, with its dark heartwood and light sapwood, was another admired speciality.

Birch, of course, was one of the most popular, and the best. A light coloured wood of very uniform consistency, it tends not to crack much and is easy to work with, and the spackling in the wood giving a nice effect. Manitoba maple, found as far north as Saskatoon, has distinctive red streaks, which are produced because of fungus. This particular tree was coveted for its burls, which were often used to make bowls and other valuable pieces not otherwise accessible to the early pioneers.

Caragana was introduced about 1902 from Asia, so this wood was used only later to make items like bells, goblets and candlesticks. Chokecherry, saskatoon, crabapple, hawthorn, buffaloberry, wild plum, basswood (which was imported from Manitoba), and hackberry, were also used to a lesser degree. Another import, Siberian elm, although a choice wood known for its beauty, was found in shelterbelts towards the latter part of the period. The Siberian elm, although not particularly distinctive at that time, was excellent for woodturning.[25]

Carved pedestal bowl with lid, unknown woodworker

Around the Qu'Appelle Valley today there are at least twenty different kinds of woods available.[26] Some were imported in the early 1900s and not all of them would be suitable for furniture building, but many, like caragana, low prairie cedar and chokecherry woods, could be used for smaller objects. Lilac, sometimes compared to ivory,[27] had limited usage and therefore was not popular. Wide diameter pieces in 12 to 14 inch lengths were required for turning, and many of these woods were too small for any other substantial type of crafting.

Basswood, found in Ontario and eastern Manitoba was desired for carving. Burr oak, generally found all over Manitoba, extended into Saskatchewan approximately to Broadview. A heavy hard wood that cracks easily, it was sought because of its striking colour.

Then there were, of course, the willows. Diamond willow, although sometimes difficult to find, was a nice specialty. Diamond willow "carving" became a popular prairie craft. This species was found mainly around sloughs and along creek and riverbanks. Although gnarled, twisted and full of knotholes, the toughness of the wood made it suitable for fence posts, walking canes and legs for tables and chairs, as well as an assortment of

Ranch '76 "Lazy Susan" table used at the headquarters of the ranch at Crane Lake to seat 15 men and was probably made by one of the ranchers.[28]

oddities that likely adorned pioneer shacks. In the early years a jackknife was often the only tool available for scraping the bark off the limbs to reveal the rough diamond shapes beneath. Other knowledgeable wood-workers may have used particular chisels suitable for the task. Frequently, the finish for diamond willow items consisted of a light sanding to smooth the contours, followed by hand polishing, although varnish, and even shoe polish has been used to some extent.[29]

Another popular method of creating furniture and household artifacts involved the use of buffalo, elk, deer, and moose horns. These items were particularly favoured from 1860 to 1900 in Europe and North America.[30] Stools, chairs and hatracks were the most common items. Sometimes the horns served as decoration or armrests rather than the functional part of a chair, with wood used for the seat and legs. Usually, these articles were padded and covered with cloth and occasionally the horns were carved. Prime examples of these types of chairs are located at the Kindersley Museum and the Old Timers' Museum at Maple Creek.

Although some of the craftspeople lived along the rail lines and could afford to import or purchase woods from outside their immediate areas, many chose to use woods available locally, which of course required careful preparation before it could be used to any degree of success. The aspect of aging wood in preparation for building was lengthy. Often the process involved painstaking selection, cutting, stacking, turning, and drying that lasted a year or more. Sometimes the outcome was disappointing when the wood cracked at the first touch of a saw blade or carving tool. At other times the results were overwhelmingly positive.

Elevation, humidity and temperature played a role in the success of aging wood and the results of the condition of the furniture after it was made. Artisans soon learned, if they hadn't known already, that wood is best turned when green and then dried slowly.[31] Householders also discovered in a hurry that cabinets and other items made on the prairies were longer lasting than their counterparts from the east that fell apart in the drier climate of the west.

There were also those woodworkers who became excellent scavengers. Although not necessarily considered masters at their trade, they were skilled and inventive. Some might even be considered outrageous and a tribute to folk art today. They scrounged crates from items delivered by trains, those that came to implement dealers, or from apple, orange or cheese boxes. Resourceful, they were almost totally self-sufficient, sometimes providing bare necessities for their neighbours when their personal needs were met.

Buffalo horn chair by Melvin Ziegler, who lived south of Maple Creek

TOOLS AND SHOPS

One of the most significant items local woodworkers made were their own tools. In many cases they brought a limited selection with them from their home countries, but once on the prairies they usually couldn't afford to purchase additional ones. There were also those who had never attempted to make furniture for themselves before and didn't possess any tools. Usually from lack of choice, they resorted to making their own hand tools which proved satisfactory to a fault.

Several resourceful woodworkers even made their own lathes which accommodated the making of more decorative features, such as candlesticks, goblets, furniture legs, and other ornamental additions. Most fashioned their own planes and some, like Olaf Pearson, also created metal carving designs, latches and hinges.

Many of the woodworkers had their own workshops on their farms, although there were several who worked on smaller items or did carvings at the kitchen table by lantern light during the winter months. A select few operated businesses from their home farms, while one or two had their own established businesses in a local town.

Lathe made by Wm Korchak of Whitebeech (See Krochak in Individual Woodworkers for more info)

Artifacts

Most of the settlers resorted to making whatever they needed for themselves, or turned to their talented family members and neighbours for assistance. Generally homesteaders adapted themselves to their needs, fending as best as they could with what they had at hand, producing

Spoons made by Adolf Steinke of Kelstern (Located in the Swift Current Museum)

sometimes crude, but serviceable items. However, there were many wood-workers that had previous training of some sort or another, and who excelled in various areas of expertise with wood, creating furnishings and accessories of striking note.

Woodworkers such as these found themselves in constant demand to supply household effects from tables, chairs, beds, cupboards, desks, and wardrobes, to more decorative features such as wall accents and picture frames, as well as the likes of trinket, sewing and handkerchief boxes. Although most items were what one would expect immigrants to need, a wide variety of artifacts were made including games, musical instruments, picture frames, sewing baskets, and other decorative features. Caring grandparents, who had more time to pursue this type of craft making, often made toys.[32]

Church paraphernalia was also popular, as every district on the prairies claimed several denominations, and one mustn't forget the ever-important coffins. There was no shortage of work for the adept and determined.

STYLES

One of the most interesting aspects about any group of settlers who came to the province is that they all had specific styles that can be attributed to their own nationalities, although, because several of the eastern European countries bordered one another, their styles sometimes crossed over. However, with a little practice, the distinctive imprints are easy to identify in a generalized way, and at times, additional scrutinizing will reveal individual woodworkers within each nationality group.

Doukhobor frame

For instance, Doukhobor pieces often have a tulip design featured as a cut-out, an applied decoration or as an inlay, whether on a table or a picture frame.[33] This motif was carried throughout other components in the lives of the Doukhobors, even onto the eaves of their homes. And assuredly, all the individual men within a Doukhobor community would have used the design extensively. As well, Doukhobor furniture usually has a denser look than Mennonite furniture which is lighter in colour and has very straight simple lines.

"Mennonite furniture is basically Germanic," says noted collector, Lindsay Anderson.[34] "It is very well thought out, very well proportioned, very utilitarian, because there is no mistaking what the piece of furniture was made for. It was a functional piece of furniture."

Basically simple plain boxes, Mennonite furniture is easily recognizable. Many of the cupboards have removable bottoms and tops,[35] making them easier to move and utilize. Doukhobor and Ukrainian furniture, on the other hand, according to Anderson, "sort of leave the realm of actually being furniture and start to get a little more sculptural. The actual function of it almost becomes debatable. It seems not as well thought out, not very practical overall in most respects."

Mennonite dresser

Of all the nationality groups, the Ukrainians and Doukhobors were the only ones who made long benches. Sometimes these trestle benches had backs, but more often not. They were located along two walls and usually used when company came.[36] Traditionally, Ukrainians didn't make corner cupboards, although some do exist.[37]

"Ukrainian furniture has little pieces coming off the sides or bases, such as cornices, so the idea of using up what is called 'negative spaces' sort of became a way they could express their artistic preference," says Anderson.

Quarter columns and arching doors can sometimes distinguish pieces made by Polish woodworkers. This is similar to Czechoslovakian-type furniture, most notably that of Vacla Yechny, a man who worked in the Esterhazy area. Austrian-Germanic items have a heavier darker appearance, and typical "s"and "c" scrolled doors, while English and Swedish artifacts are usually made from oak and lighter woods and have intricate carvings on the surface, although each with their own particular style.[38]

WOMEN'S ROLES

While the women certainly played an important and usually over-looked supportive role, the majority of the woodworkers and furniture makers, according to findings in this survey, appear to have been men. The women remained in the background, and surprisingly were often not allowed to assist their spouses in any way, not even with the surface finishing work of articles. In part, this may have been due to the women being totally occupied with the domestic side of life, as well as being engaged in helping with the outdoor farm activities and chores. Their support allowed their menfolk the freedom to pursue their talents uninhibited. This was a sign of the times, not wholly unexpected, but a passive cooperative role-play to the fullest.

One would like to think that, at the very least, most women had some voice in the design of an article, particularly if they requested something for their own use. And to be fair, there were those woodworkers, like John Danchilla from Canora, who worked at the kitchen table and welcomed watchful eyes or appreciated input and ideas from their spouses, but this did not occur often.

One outstanding exception to this seeming lack of female wood-workers was Mademoiselle Onésime Dorval, who was also a lay mission-ary nun, painter, and the first certified teacher in the province.[39] She lived at Battleford for a time, and later at Batoche during the time of the Northwest Rebellion, where she built plank sidewalks and created the majority of her wood artifacts. There may have been other women who worked with wood from necessity, but so far they have not come to light.

FAMILY PARTICIPATION

In many cases the children of the woodworkers weren't involved in their father's work either, and the skills not passed on. There were anomalies as in the instances of the McGuirls of Moosomin and the Nostbakkens of Aneroid, who imparted their knowledge willingly to the next generation. Sometimes the children puttered around on their own, and maybe in later years developed an interest in working with wood, but in most situations the offspring were not allowed near their father's work. The only excep-tion might have been in the cleaning of the workshops.

Russian plane

Hutterite collection from 1950s

ETHNIC GROUPS

There also seem to be groups of different nationalities where specific names have not been attributed to particular pieces. For instance, the Doukhobors are often considered as a group rather than as individual woodworkers, because of the nature of their socially tight-knit colonies.[40] However, there are some names that stand out such as Wasyl Zubenkoff, who produced furniture and frames in the Kamsack/Veregin region.[41] There were additional pockets where the Doukhobors settled in the province, probably each with predominantly known woodworkers. Eventually however, many of the Doukhobors moved to British Columbia in the Grand Forks/Castlegar area and today only a few select pieces of woodwork remain.[42]

The Mennonites are also a group that produced distinctive works of art. They came from Manitoba during a large influx between 1903 and 1906 and settled in the general Swift Current and Rosthern areas. Although they lived in several colonies, they were of a different style and individual woodworkers, like Mr. Neustaeter and Mr. Schoenfeld, had their own businesses within each community.[43]

Hutterite toiletry shelf

Although the Hutterites have been industrious woodworkers, their work was not reviewed for this study because they didn't arrive in the province until the 1950s.[44] Today they continue to produce similar styles of woodwork that can be traced back several decades, but they brought most of the older pieces still in existence with them when they came to Saskatchewan. In addition, they were actually known for their basketry. Woodworking was not their predominant skill, but one they adopted when they arrived in North America.[45]

FIRST NATIONS

Though the First Nations populations on the prairies were enterprising in activities like building canoes and travois, weaving willow baskets, carving pipes, and doing birchbark biting creations, other woodworking projects by this group seem to be limited due in part to their lack of need for such items. They made furniture to a certain extent at times, but it was

Dugout canoe in the museum in Prince Albert

undoubtedly influenced by the invasion of European culture. Therefore, their work was not pursued in depth within the confines of this research. In fact, the focus for this study had to be narrowed down considerably because of the sheer numbers of noteworthy people to include, and many worthwhile craftspeople and elements are only mentioned briefly.

SUMMATION

According to Lindsay Anderson, in comparison to the whole population, the English, Irish, and Scottish groups made virtually nothing in the way of wood products, even though sixty per cent of the people who settled on the prairies were English speaking. The Eastern Europeans made the most, especially certain ethnic groups during particular times.[46] Although more information might come to light if a comparable study were done in Manitoba and Alberta, preliminary evidence shows that on a regional basis several predominant craftspeople existed in Manitoba, but Alberta never saw much in the way of crafts.[47]

Saskatchewan, it seems, was the prevalent settling area for woodworkers and furniture makers of prominence. Where this researcher might have expected to find only two or three dozen distinctive woodworkers or furniture makers, this study revealed an astounding one hundred and twenty individuals, with perhaps a significant number yet to be discovered.

Certainly, there were others as the years progressed, and the majority of these known craftspeople continued to produce into the 1930s and 1940s, and beyond, often right until their deaths. However, with the onset of electricity and influences by Sears' and Eaton's catalogues, the handcrafted art as it was known at the onset of immigration began to dwindle.

After the Second World War, the industry never recovered. Today there are a number of skilled craftsmen and hobbyists at work creating wood artifacts, but the discipline as it was known at the turn of the century has largely died out.

Those who produced the most items were John McGuirl, Joachim Pilon and Olaf Pearson, with Pearson creating the most unusual individual

Well-known artists like Sam Spencer who did this carved piece are not included as he worked well beyond the years contained in the scope of this book.

ones, and McGuirl perhaps being the most prolific builder of commercial type furniture. All the woodworkers during that time, however, deserve acknowledgement for their achievements. Even though most items were never signed or identified in any way, nor dates determined with any accuracy, these craftspeople left their mark in history.

True, these talented people simply did what they had to do, but they did it with perseverance and fortitude. There were so few items available to inhabitants when they first arrived that they had to start virtually from scratch, reproducing everything a family or business person needed, with the majority of pieces being constructed for use in their own homes. Although there were those who made ornate pieces, most resorted to simple lines and straightforward creations that were serviceable and durable, and quickly made for immediate use.

Regardless of the reason behind the work, these diligent woodworkers persevered. Thanks to people like Peter Mandziuk, this art has not been entirely lost to us. A folk artist, he is very knowledgeable in this craft from the past. He became consciously aware of its significance in the 1950s when he first began collecting the artifacts, long before any one else did.[48] Through his efforts, and those of subsequent collectors, many of these items have been preserved that otherwise might not have been.

Perhaps one might assume that auctioneers who are in contact with these types of artifacts continually would have some knowledge or awareness, but this has not been the case. According to Lindsay Anderson, "auctioneers don't know and don't particularly care where pieces came from or who made them, and generally most people you talk to about these pieces don't know either." This has contributed to a general lack of knowledge about woodworkers and their work.

Although there seems to have been a shroud of mystery about this topic among the general populace for several decades, this art form is one that touches countless people regardless of their different cultural backgrounds. Nearly every family in Saskatchewan has at least one piece of wood furniture or other wood artifacts in their home. Often these pieces are considered heirlooms, more valuable than money in the settling of a will. Most owners are proud of their wood-crafted items, but few people know the history of their pieces, and fewer still under-

Carvings found in the museum in Prince Albert

stand that many of these artifacts were made right here in Saskatchewan by very talented woodworkers.

One of the reasons that Saskatchewan is rich in cultural diversity is the artistic ability and craftsmanship that our forefathers brought here with them. Not only is it important to impart this knowledge and preserve our culture, but it also provides a valuable connecting link between our ancestors and us. Certainly there is importance in recording as much as possible about these gifted artisans, and they deserve recognition for their incredible accomplishments, done in one of the most difficult of times.

This book then is a starting point, and perhaps because of it more of these gifted artisans will come to light, and these incredible wood artifacts will continue to be an enduring reminder of who we are and where we came from.

ENDNOTES

1. Derived from an overview of the research conducted by the author.

2. There were also other posts established during this time: La Loche, Ile à la Crosse,

Green Lake, La Ronge, and Frog Portage. Richards, J.H. and Fung, K.I., Editors, *Atlas of Saskatchewan,* (Saskatchewan: University of Saskatchewan, 1969), p. 16.

3. Ibid. p. 16.

4. Ibid. p. 16. "Pond is responsible for the first factually-based map on the western interior and the North-West...." (Although inaccurate in detail.) Trained surveyor, Philip Turnor conducted explorations and produced accurate information and preparation of maps. He also trained Peter Fiddler and David Thompson.

5. Prince Albert Historical Society, *Voice of the People,* "James Nisbet Letters and Papers," 1984, p. 9. Nisbet, a Presbyterian minister, has been credited as the founder of Prince Albert. According to an article "'The Most Good to the Indians': The Reverend James Nisbet and the Prince Albert Mission," in Saskatchewan History, p.34-35 by W. D. (Bill) Smiley. Nisbet used his skills as a carpenter to help build churches and schools in the Red River communities of Manitoba, and he also built many pieces of furniture in Prince Albert. Note: Stanley Mission was established in 1854, and is generally considered by experts to be the first permanent community in Saskatchewan.

6. Ibid. "Mrs. Margaret McKenzie," p. 51. William Miller was "one of the earliest and best known of early settlers." (Margaret was one of William Miller's daughters.)

7. Notes from Frank Korvemaker interview.

8. On July 15, 1870 the province of Manitoba and the Northwest Territories became part of Canada. Throughout the 1870s and onward into the early 1900s negotiations of treaties resulting in the creation of reservations, and the land surveys parceling the region in viable tracts influenced the increase of early settlement. *A Historical Atlas of Canada,* Kerr, D. G.G. (Canada: Toronto, 1960, Thomas Nelson & Sons (Canada) Ltd.), p.56-58.

9. *Atlas of Saskatchewan,* p. 17. "The choice of Battleford (1876) as first seat of the territorial government, as well as a police post and point on the Dominion telegraph and proposed Pacific railway, accounted for the immediate growth of that centre."

10. Taken from interview with Frank Korvemaker.

11. *Atlas of Saskatchewan,* p.17 Section on "Settlement after 1901."

12. The Parleys of the Grenfell area were noted for travelling to homestead sites and being able to construct a simple shanty in one day. (Taken from interview notes with George Vipond, a relative of the Parleys.)

13. Work done by Stevens[on] has been found in the area, but very little information can be obtained, including his first name, although it may possibly be William.

14. According to Sallie Peirson, Director of the Estevan Museum, interviewed July 17, 1994.

15. There were essential requirements outlined for "proving" a homestead, which often included clearing a certain amount of land within a certain time frame.

16. Broadview Pioneer History Society, *Story of Broadview and Area: Centennial Tribute, Oakshela, Broadview, Percival, 1882-1982,* (Altone, Manitoba: Friesen Printers, 1982), p.11.

17. Derived from compilation of the author's research.

18. Information from Louw, H. J. "Demarcation Disputes Between English Carpenters and Joiners from the Sixteenth to the Eighteenth Century," *Construction History,* Vol.5, 1989, p. 3-20.

19. William(?) Stevens[on] has been rather an elusive woodworker to track down. Although his work seems to be known, nothing much in the way of information has come to light, and even if this is his proper name is not known.

20. Derived from the author's research.

21. Ibid.

22. John Kort is a Shelterbelt Biologist/Agroforester with the Shelter Belt Centre at Indian Head, Saskatchewan.

23. According to John Kort: Populus deltoides—the plains cottonwood is found in southern Saskatchewan, while Populus tremulous (trembling aspen) is found throughout the province.

24. According to John Kort, it is not found in the middle of the prairies.

25. According to Frank Sudol, in the PFRA information pamphlet *Wood Turning.*

26. There is a display in the Whitewood Museum, assembled by Joe Callin, which gives examples of seventeen woods found on his farm, plus three found in the Qu'Appelle Valley. They are: spruce, pine, ash, apple, maple, oak, paper birch, willow, pincherry, lilac, silver willow, caragana, honeysuckle, plum, Russian olive, red willow, black birch, chokecherry, willow, and hawthorn. There may also be others available such as elm.

27. According to T.A. Mack of Lumsden in the article "Early Furniture" by Muriel Clipsham in *The Canadian Collector,* July/August 1973, p. 34-35.

28. The townsite of Gull Lake was once part of the 130 thousand acre '76 Ranch. The

Ranch house built in 1899 is now used as the Gull Lake School Division office.

29. Condensed from an article entitled "Early Furniture" by Muriel Clipsham in the *The Canadian Collector,* July/August 1973, p. 34-35.

30. Ibid.

31. Frank Sudol comments in PFRA pamphlet *Wood Turning.*

32. Notes from conversations with Lindsay Anderson.

33. The tulip design is traditionally a religious symbol representing the Holy Trinity, however, this is not necessarily the reason the Doukhobors use it. According to Lindsay Anderson, who has spoken with wide variety of Doukhobor people, they have no knowledge of why they use this and other symbols.

34. Ibid.

35. Interview with Doug Bentham of Saskatoon.

36. Ibid.

37. Ibid. He came across at least one such cupboard, but says this is quite unusual.

38. Noted by Lindsay Anderson and Ralph Jarotski.

39. Mlle. Dorval file at Batoche.

40. There were three blocks or colonies with over 500,000 acres of land set aside for the Doukhobors in Saskatchewan: two colonies in the Yorkton/Canora/Pelly region, and one in the Saskatoon/Blaine Lake area. They set up sixty-one villages, with the one at Veregin perhaps being the most famous because it was named after their leader. 7,500 Doukhobors immigrated in 1898-99. *Pictorial History of the Doukhobors* by Koozma J. Tarasoff. (Saskatoon, Canada: Prairie Books Department, *The Western Producer,* Modern Press, 1969), p. 67.

41. Wasyl Zubenkoff, possibly came with the first wave of settlers in 1896. He also taught woodworking in the area, and today one of his frames might reach upwards of $10,000, according to Ralph Jarotski, a collector from Canora.

42. Ibid., p. 14. They were evicted from 250,000 acres of choice farmland in 1907 by the new Minister of the Interior. Information was also derived from interviews with Lindsay Anderson.

Note also that many Doukhobor pieces were shipped out of the province to astute collectors.

43. Interview with Hugh Henry, curator at the Swift Current Museum.

44. Taken from interview with Susan Hoffer and the internally-produced history book at the Estuary River Colony. The Hutterites didn't begin to arrive until 1952.

45. This was noted in a conversation with Lindsay Anderson of Regina.

46. The Doukhobors eventually went to B.C., the Mennonites originally settled mostly in Manitoba before venturing to the neighbouring province, while the Ukrainians lived predominantly in Saskatchewan.

47. According to Lindsay Anderson, who travelled, researched and actively sought furniture as a collector in the three Prairie Provinces.

48. Peter Mandziuk and his wife began collecting ethnic furniture in the late 1950s.

Major
WOODWORKERS

Onésime Dorval
(1845-1932)

Onésime Dorval's pursuits as a prairie woodworker were only incidental to the entirety of her extraordinary life, yet this was one of the many talents at which she excelled. In spite of being delicate physically in her youth, Dorval's feisty spirit compelled her to venture forth in 1877 to not only become the first qualified teacher in the great Canadian North-West, but a pioneer lay missionary nun, an artist, and a woodworker in her own right.

Born on August 3, 1845, her parents lived on a humble farm near Ste. Scholastique, Quebec. Although her father, Ignace Dorval, farmed for his livelihood, he was perhaps a carpenter at heart. At least, he supplemented his income in this manner. Of her mother, Esther Brunette, little is known.[1] One can only surmise that she was a hardy woman with great forbearance to allow her daughter to be parted from the family early in her life.

In 1849 when Onésime was four, the Dorval family established themselves at St. Jerome. Six years later, she first learned courage and independence, when her parents sent her back to Ste. Scholastique alone.

There she became a boarder, studying at the convent of the Sisters of the Holy Cross. A good student, in time she became employed as a substitute teacher, while she completed her studies.

During the later years of her professional development, Dorval returned to St. Jerome where she sought lodging at the Convent of the Sisters of St. Anne, who had recently established themselves there. While in attendance at the convent, she obtained her "First Class" teacher's diploma, passing exams in "deductive reasoning, grammar, literature, arithmetic, history, algebra, and geometry."[2] This allowed her to teach in all the school "models" of the jurisdiction.

Still, as a young teacher, Onésime's health became precarious,[3] and although she had a strong desire to become a nun, the congregation thought her admission was undesirable. Not deterred, she decided to do her apprenticeship in the United States. Consequently, she entered the Good Shepherd Monastery in New York City. During her stay there she became extremely ill. The exact type of illness has never been determined. Although taking the vows to enable her to become a nun were no longer possible, she had benefitted by learning to speak English fluently, which proved to be a great asset in her future.

Mlle Dorval (back far left) with her students at St. Vital School at Battleford
(Photo courtesy Sisters of the Presentation of Marie Rivier Academy Collection, Prince Albert)

Forced to return to Quebec because of her poor health, Dorval prayed fervently to be cured from her physical sickness, promising that if she were healed, she would dedicate the rest of her life to God's will. Her prayers were answered, she believed, through the intervention of the spirit of St. Ignace de Loyola, and she was miraculously healed. After her recuperation, she decided to pursue her teaching career, and on May 5, 1875, she received her teaching certificate "L'École Modele" from Montreal.[4] Shortly after this, she approached an Oblate priest, Father Lacombe, O.M.I., to ask him how she could best realize her promise of serving God. He was recruiting teachers for Bishop Vital Grandin, the local Ordinary of the Diocese of St. Albert, near present-day Edmonton.[5] At the time the North-West was opening up and Msgr. Grandin needed teachers and missionaries. Dorval's adventurous spirit heeded the call, and she made plans to go to the prairies, intending to teach the children that resided there.

Dorval's compassion for children shone early, and by this time she had adopted a young girl, known only as Mary. Mary, as well as one of Dorval's young nieces who also wanted to work in the missions, accompanied her on July 20, 1877 when she left her village in Quebec for the vast North-West.[6]

Dorval and her companions arrived on the rain-drenched streets of Winnipeg early on the morning of August 5, where they were met by Msgr. Taché. He escorted them to the Ste. Marie mission to await the arrival of Bishop Vital Grandin.

Msgr. Grandin duly appeared a week later, but he was leaving for a two-year sojourn to France to regain his health. He feared there would be problems with some of the Ojibway people on the prairies, and he persuaded Dorval to wait in the area for his return.[7] Disgruntled, but accepting her fate, she agreed.

In the course of Dorval's stay at the Ste. Marie mission, her niece left for a visit to the mission of Father Camper at Lake Manitoba. While the young companion was gone, Dorval sent her own child to be cared for by the Sisters, but Mary was distressed at the separation from her adoptive mother. Dorval was also dissatisfied with her own life, wanting to do more worthwhile work while biding her time for Msgr. Grandin's return.

She was relieved when, at the beginning of the new year, Father St. Pierre of Baie St. Paul (near St. François-Xavier) asked her to come and teach in his parish situated on the south bank of the far-reaching Assiniboine River. With the consent of her superiors Dorval agreed, and the little family group from Quebec was once again reunited.

The inhabitants of Baie St. Paul received Dorval enthusiastically; they had never had a schoolteacher before. They soon elected to build her a new schoolhouse. In due course, the classroom was established near the church on the bank of the river, and Dorval was content living in the community, where her teaching efforts and kindness were appreciated. She was also delighted to find that one of the residents was a former classmate of hers from Ste. Scholastique.

During the two years she devoted herself to teaching the Métis and French Canadians inhabitants at Baie St. Paul. When Msgr. Grandin finally reappeared in Manitoba, he persuaded Dorval to continue to St. Albert where he was headed. She agreed, but insisted on finishing the few months of her contract at Baie St. Paul. She followed Grandin at the end of the school term in June of 1880, after retrieving her adopted child Mary from the east where she had been visiting.[8] Dorval was also to see her grandparents one last time.

The trip west took two and a half months, travelling in a caravan of nineteen Red River carts and oxen under the charge of Louis Chatelaine. Father Florent Hert met Dorval's weary entourage in Battleford, where she spent one night in a miserable cabin, before continuing on her way.[9] She arrived at St. Albert on September 7. There she found lodging with the Grey Nuns, but because of lack of space in their convent, she left almost immediately for St. Anne's Lake, north of Edmonton, where she had asked to spend the winter.

While there, the young missionary teacher taught French, English and arithmetic to two students, whose father was studying Latin under Msgr. Grandin. Then on February 2, 1881, Dorval took her vows of poverty, chastity and obedience as a lay Franciscan missionary. Her adopted daughter also received confirmation during this same Epiphany service, which a visiting Msgr. Grandin conducted. After the ceremony he promised the young girl, who no doubt found life there bleak and lonely, that they would move to St. Albert.

Accordingly, they left the following spring. Upon arriving in St. Laurent, Dorval found conditions appalling. "The school of the place vegetated since its foundation because of the incompetence of the teachers, followed by the indifference of the Métis," she wrote in her journal.[10]

Dorval, through her tact, kindness and zeal, quickly organized the school. Presumably, she also wielded

Mlle Onésime Dorval with her protegé Miss Darmous (standing) (Photo courtesy Sisters of the Presentation of Marie Rivier Academy Collection, Prince Albert)

a hammer, utilizing a more practical physical approach in establishing a stable institution. Soon she was teaching thirty students.[11]

Later, she also initiated a prayer corner in the trunk of a tree in the yard, where she would gather her students to pray to the Rosary in the company of Father Fourmond and the staff of the mission. She also helped Fourmond in his charity works. Always devout, the following year Dorval was allowed by Bishop Grandin to make perpetual vows, adding to her previous ones, the vow of perseverance. And there is little doubt, she had plenty of this important characteristic.

In June of 1883, four sisters from the Sisters of the Faithful Companions of Jesus came to replace Dorval, and to set up a boarding school. Although she stayed to train them for several weeks, Dorval accepted a teaching position in Battleford. By now her adopted daughter Mary was also old enough to attend a boarding school, and the girl was sent to Prince Albert where she would stay at the convent of the Faithful Companions of Jesus, who were also establishing a school there. Mary was to be their first boarder.[12]

Dorval left for Battleford, the capital of the North-West, the last week of August in 1883 with Father Bigonesse. She also took a cow and two hens, which had been offered to her by Father André, perhaps his way of apologizing for his earlier attempts at tricking her into staying in his community. At any rate, the livestock was a great comfort to Dorval as the mission of Battleford was very poor.

After her arrival, she resided temporarily with the Rivard family.[13] On September 3, 1883, Dorval opened St. Vital School, a log building on the south side of Battle River at the foot of the hill near where Government House then stood.[14] She was instantly challenged with making herself understood to the five or six Métis students who spoke only Cree. Another student, the eight-year-old Irish son of Sergeant Burke, the bugler of the garrison, joined a short time later. Luckily, he spoke English.

Dorval took such difficulties as these in stride, and went on to establish one of the finest bilingual systems of education in the Territories.[15] She was known "for combining discipline with kindness, and her academic background was far in advance of her time."[16]

By the spring of 1884, she and Father Bigonesse moved into their new house beside the church. However, it wasn't finished, and they were forced to complete it themselves. By this time Dorval, if she hadn't been already, proved herself adept with a hammer. No small feat, it was just one more thing that Dorval took in stride—another task to which she was not unaccustomed.

At every mission she'd ever encountered, she'd had to be resourceful, inventive and tenacious to make everything work, and this venture was no different. Cheerfully she undertook to rectify and construct any necessary components to make her life bearable there. This accomplished, she set about successfully organizing the academic end of the school.

The next obstacle in her life was the outbreak of the Northwest Rebellion in 1885. During the two months of the insurrection she sought refuge behind the palisade of the local police barracks with the other members of the population. Dorval admitted to feeling insecure staying in the fort, and recounted the suffering of those terrifying days in her journal. Courage once again in hand, however, she reopened the school on May 26, and continued teaching at Battleford, revitalizing St. Vital school, which became recognized as among the best Catholic schools in the North-West.

In 1893, a bigger house was built when the Sisters of the Assumption arrived from Nicolet to establish a convent. As they did not hold valid teaching certificates Dorval had to remain with them for three more years, until they received their certification from the Normal School in Calgary.

Then in July of 1896, Dorval left Battleford. The ladies of the area gave her a settee as a parting gift, which she took with her.[17] She intended to return to the mission at St. Laurent. However, that parish was no longer the one she'd previously known. Most of the families had departed for the mission of St. Antoine at Batoche. Dorval also went to Batoche where she willingly dedicated her services under Father Julien Moulin. Here she taught her beloved Métis for eighteen years in what became known as School District No. 1.

A more elderly Mlle Dorval
(Photo courtesy Sisters of the Presentation of Marie Rivier Academy Collection, Prince Albert)

Dorval once again set to constructing, decorating, and organizing the mission into a homey, yet respectful atmosphere. She added curtains to the windows and a rug to the floor. Dividing a room behind the parsonage, she assembled a "wall" of single cartons, which she attached together and hung with a tapestry. Students were amazed that she'd even constructed an entry door.[18] One area facilitated a personal space for Dorval, and the other sufficed as a kitchen.

It is believed that this was the time when she also built the impressive kitchen table. Although somewhat crude by today's standards, it was a solid functional piece of furniture, complete with dovetail joints. As well, Dorval used wooden pegs, rather than nails to hold the table together.

Adaptable as always, "she also made for herself a very narrow sidewalk, long narrow slats of wood on cross bars, to go to and from the church to the parsonage's back door."[19] At various spots along this board walkway, she planted her favourite flowers—pansies.

These pansies were possibly the inspiration for the birchbark flowers that Dorval fashioned. One of her students, Octavie Pilon, sometimes assisted Mlle Dorval in making these flowers, and Dorval often had the children paint them as part of their art curriculum. Sister Gerardin Chamberland, one of her students in 1911, in particular recalls them.

> "Among her many talents for creating pretty objects out of nothing, we admired the flowers, roses, violets, etc., she carved in wood with a pocket knife and then painted the desired colour. In our youthful eyes, these artistic pieces were real wonders. I remember among other 'bouquets' she thus fabricated two small crowns of violets, which for a long time ornamented the church walls on both sides of the altar."[20]

Dorval also later made a miniature bellows, which she later presented as a gift to Octavie Pilon. She constructed this from doeskin, glued to a varnished wooden front and back. A tapered cylindrical metal nosepiece was fastened to the body with wrapped doeskin, and a heart-shaped decoration on the front has the word SOUVENIR inscribed on it at the centre. Three flowers and a leaf are carved above this, and one below. On the back centre is a diamond-shaped wooden piece upon which Dorval carved a starburst.[21]

Always resourceful, Dorval created a cross from odds and ends. Beginning with a willow branch, she placed it into a discarded object that may have been a doorknob or some other chunk of wood that had been carved using a lathe. She adorned it with a tiny metal medallion and Christ figure. This probably stood on her personal altar.

Although it's not known when she took up painting, according to oral history Dorval used no brushes, because there were none available. Instead she dipped her fingernails in paint or ink to sketch scenes of the surrounding area. One such painting still hangs on the kitchen wall in the parsonage at Batoche National Historic Park. Perhaps its frame was even made by her, although there is no way of confirming this. The painting itself depicts the Batoche mission at the time Dorval lived there.

Successes with her students such as this seem to have been reward enough for Dorval. Teachers at that time made $50 per month, but Dorval had long since made arrangements for turning over all of her earnings to the Oblate fathers in exchange for her care in retirement. She had a great respect for the Oblate fathers and the priests with whom she worked.

She also practised the poverty part of her vows to a degree "to which was an example to many of us modern nuns."[22] According to Sister Chamberland, "she was always dressed in a long black dress with a belt and a cape which covered her and came down her shoulders. When she came to visit us she was covered by a long cape instead of a coat and wore a simple black hat without ornament." Apparently she was also the picture of modesty while entering or descending from a vehicle.

Dorval had a determined nature, full of self-discipline and forbearance, but she loved laughing and joking with people. She's also known to play the harmonium quite skilfully.[23] She often assisted at communion services, and afterwards cared for the children, bringing them slices of buttered bread and glasses of milk or water.

According to Sister Chamberland, many often commented about Dorval, "'How can she have so much authority with the children as she never gets angry!'"[24] Chamberland goes on to explain in her letter that Dorval "was never impatient with us, who were mischievous to the point of nearly demolishing the wall of her room...."

Dorval weathered all types of behaviour and problems through-

Mlle Dorval in later years
(Provincial Archives of Alberta photo:
O.B. 4104)

43

out her years at Batoche, fondly recalling those days that eventually came to an end. In 1914, when Father Moulin retired and left the mission, Dorval left for Aldina, near the Muskeg Reserve in north-central Saskatchewan, where she taught for one year, feeling that she was needed more there.

Earlier in the year, on February 21, she had been granted an official Province of Saskatchewan "Professional First Class Certificate" for teaching. Although she'd acquired one in Quebec, and one for the North-West Territories, she no doubt felt it prudent to have the appropriate one from the newly-established province.

On October 5, 1915 Father Henri Delmas (Silmas),[25] an Oblate priest, invited her to retire with the Sisters of the Presentation of Mary at St. Michael's Indian Residential School in Duck Lake. Although Dorval accepted, the following year, at the age of 70, she came out of retirement to resume teaching duties of the Métis at St. Laurent.

Six years later, now earning $1200 per year, Dorval finally retired for

Mlle Dorval retired and lived out her last days at St. Michael's School at Duck Lake (Companion unknown)
Photo courtesy Sisters of the Presentation of Marie Rivier Academy Collection, Prince Albert)

good in 1921, but her interest in children never subsided.[26] When the children came to visit her, she'd gather them on little wooden stools around her, and tell them about the "good old days," regaling them of tales of her days during the Northwest Rebellion, and her trials and tribulations in an untamed wilderness, and uncivilized society.

Dorval painting

Onésime Dorval deserves to be remembered as an extraordinary and diversified individual. She endured beyond belief in today's world, especially considering her delicate constitution in her youth. She seems to have been admired by all who came in contact with her, for her remarkable memory, sound judgement, her cheerful disposition and edifying piety.

Dedicated and perseverant all of her days, Dorval never shirked any of her duties, giving far more of herself than was ever required. From the first

Dorval cross

trained teacher to travel to the Canadian North-West, to a lay missionary nun, artist and skilful woodworker, she is certainly a person of note.

She passed away peacefully at St. John's Hospital, Rosthern, on Saturday, December 10, 1932, at the age of 87.[27] She is buried in the Duck Lake cemetery near St. Michael's School, with the Sisters of Presentation of Mary.

Today Dorval's pieces can be found in the Environment Canada Parks Services holdings, at the Batoche National Historic Park,

Dorval flowers

Dorval bellows
(Photo courtesy: Environments Canada,
Parks Service, 1993)

and the Duck Lake Museum. There one might see the delicate pansies carved from birchbark, the simple cross made of a twig and found objects or the kitchen table that remains as sturdy and useful today as it did when Dorval first manufactured it. There is little doubt that Onésime Dorval's spirit of ingenuity and perseverance lives on.

Dorval table

Note about photographs: Please note that some photographs in this chapter are available from several sources, including the Sisters of the Presentation of Marie Rivier Academy Collection in Prince Albert; the Provincial Archives of Alberta, Oblate Archives, Edmonton (OB. 4100, OB. 4101, OB. 4102, OB. 61, OB. 3830); and Environment Canada, Parks Services, and Batoche National Park; as well as a number of private sources. The photographs of the artifacts not noted in the text are those taken by Linda McDowell.

ENDNOTES
_____

1. One account says the family may have been known as Bellehumeur.

2. Taken from a photocopy of her teaching certificate, obtained from the Archives of Alberta in Edmonton.

3. What type of illness she had has never been determined.

4. Taken from a copy of her teaching certificate, which she obtained from the Montreal bureau.

5. Maurice Fiolleau's article, p. 1.

6. According to her journal Mary and her niece accompanied her. She had adopted Mary a few years earlier. (Also according to her journal.)

7. Some accounts say it was the Sioux that Msgr. Grandin was concerned about.

8. Although no mention is made in any of the sources, Dorval's daughter must have stayed behind on one of the visits to Quebec.

9. She left August 16, 1880.

10. According to the "Une Apostolique" article from the OMI in Edmonton.

11. Ibid. According to the article, it was during her stay that the pilgrimage to Notre-Dame from Lourdes began.

12. From *Kaleidoscope: History of the Diocese of Prince Albert,* 1991, p. 519.

13. Mr. Rivard was the contractor who built the church between the two rivers.

14. Government House is now the St. Charles Scholasticite, according to one of the small write-ups that came from the Prince Albert sisters.

15. "During her tenure she witnessed the formation of St. Vital School District No. 11 of the North-West Territories in 1886..." Page 519 *Kaleidoscope: History of the Diocese of Prince Albert,* 1991.

16. From a small article written by the Sisters of the Presentation of Mary, Diocese of Prince Albert.

17. According to an interview with Edward Bruce, Acting Supervisor, Visitor Activities, Batoche National Historic Park.

18. Description and comments from Sister Gerardin Chamberland's letter to Sister Josephine Oiullet written in 1981. Sister Chamberland was a student of Mlle Dorval's in 1911.

19. Ibid.

20. Ibid.

21. This artifact is being held at Environment Canada, Parks Service in Winnipeg, Manitoba.

22. From Sister Chamberland's letter.

23. This instrument is located in the Duck Lake Museum.

24. In a letter from Sister Chamberlain from St. Boniface, Manitoba to Sister Josephine Ouillet of Prince Albert, written in 1981.

25. In the typed copy of her journal the name is Silmas, however two subsequent write-ups, one by Quenneville, and the other one titled "Une Apostle" both say the name is Delmas, while the history book of Prince Albert. (*Kaleidoscope*) says it is Silas (clearly a typo).

26. This was in 1921.

27. *StarPhoenix* article, December 14, 1932, p. 13.

JOHN McGUIRL
(1850-1913)

JOHN McGUIRL HOLDS THE HONOUR OF BEING ONE OF THE earliest woodworkers to operate a successful, full-fledged commercial venture on the prairies. Although he died soon after the turn of the century,[1] he left a lasting legacy not to be surpassed perhaps by any other woodworker, who has since ventured to Saskatchewan.

Born on July 4, 1850, at Kingston, Ontario, McGuirl was already married and living at Merrickville by the time he decided to move west.[2] He was well-established as a woodworker of note in his home province, and his strong moral beliefs also seem to have been in place. In 1870 he is cited as being a member of both the 14th Regiment of the Prince of Wales' Own Rifles, and the Fenian Raid Veterans.[3] He also joined the Masons of Merrickville Lodge 55 in 1871. These firm convictions seemed destined to be carried later into his life on the prairies.

Although he arrived in what became known as the Stanley District near Moosomin in 1882, his wife and their three children followed the next spring.[4] They were amongst the earliest pioneers of the district, with John "among the first settlers to travel over the CPR, then under construction across the prairie."[5] He applied for a homestead[6] which he kept for several years.

During their time on the farm, his wife, Emma Julia Carter,[7] delivered a daughter, Minnie, who was supposedly the first settler's baby born in the area.[8] Although the McGuirls had a total of seven children, four of whom were born in the Moosomin area, one daughter died at a young age from an accident in 1881,[9] and a son from the influenza epidemic in 1918.[10] Minnie, along with the two older boys, James, and Charlie, were among the first children to begin their education in the Stanley District School when it opened in July of 1889.

Almost immediately after he arrived, McGuirl "opened a small carpentry shop, and built many of the first houses in the neighbourhood, the majority of the earlier arrivals then living in tents. His own house was the first gable-roofed building in the community."[11] This he built in the town of Moosomin, where the family eventually moved, although he continued to own his quarter section at least until 1905.[12]

John McGuirl's whole life seems to have been devoted to woodworking. In his native Ontario he'd had considerable training in the furniture line as well as woodworking of all kinds,[13] and soon after he established himself in the Moosomin community, McGuirl opened a furniture factory in the town. He later called it the Moosomin Planing Mill, specializing in the manufacture of church and lodge furnishings.

McGuirl planing mill (SK Archives Board: R-A19059)

McGuirl furntiure factory (SK Archives Board: R-A19061)

In the early days he employed several men in his planing mill: James Bell, Tom Rice, Charlie Draper, J.J. Scott, Louis Colvin, Charlie Burgess, and Tom Wells. Later he opened a furniture store and undertaking parlour on East Front Street in the town.[14] He also operated the local lumberyard, and began construction of sashes, doors and caskets.

Three years after his arrival, McGuirl undertook one of his biggest projects. This occurred when he was asked to superintend the construction of St. Alban's Anglican Church in Moosomin. The foundations were laid in June of 1885, and the church was dedicated in October of the same year. John McGuirl, besides being the chief architect and overseer of the building project, also "manufactured the basic furniture in the church, completing this project with the pews, in 1892."[15] Several years later, he was contracted to create a special Bishop's Chair, which still resides in the church sanctuary. This "handsome and beautifully carved chair...reported to be a work of art, was ready for Easter Sunday, 1904."[16]

One of McGuirl's greatest accomplishments was the Moosomin

Masonic Lodge, which he completely furnished about 1888. This talented woodworker created and hand-carved everything from benches, desks and chairs, to the pedestals and pillars. As well, in 1908 he dispatched some of his finest oak furniture to the Masonic Lodge in Regina, and in 1910 he shipped a carload of furniture to Indian Head for the Odd Fellow Lodge there.[17]

McGuirl's involvement with the Masons didn't end with just supplying furniture, however. McGuirl had been influential in obtaining a dispensation for the opening of the Masonic Lodge in Moosomin in 1888. Besides being one of the applicants for the Moosomin Charter, he held many offices in the local and Grand Lodges of Assiniboia, being elected to the highest offices within the power of his fellow Masons. He was Past Grand Junior Warden of the Grand Lodge of Saskatchewan (in 1908 and 1909), and Worshipful Master in 1889. He was elected to office in the Grand Lodge of Manitoba, and in 1896 was DDGM for District 8, Assiniboia. In addition, McGuirl was active in civic and legislative life of the community, in time becoming a member of the Town Council,[18] and serving a long term on the Moosomin General Hospital Board.

Of McGuirl's wife little is known, except from her obituary notice, which states that Emma was "kindly, considerate, hospitable, a typical pioneer, she was esteemed by all who knew her...an ardent church and missionary worker and a staunch member of the Presbyterian church."[19] As with so many women of that time frame, it is doubtful that Emma McGuirl ever assisted her husband directly with his woodworking. No doubt she had been supportive in many other

Speaker's Chair, Masonic Lodge, Moosomin

ways, and she seems to have been well thought of in the community. Of their offspring, several, including Charlie and James, eventually became part of the McGuirl enterprise, helping their father produce many fine pieces of furniture, including those for the Saskatchewan government.[20]

Detail of Speaker's Chair, Masonic Lodge, Moosomin.

Although it can't be proven without a doubt, there is a strong indication that McGuirl created the Speaker's Chair that now resides in the Saskatchewan Legislature, which once belonged to Thomas MacNutt, M.L.A. for Saltcoats Constituency. He was the first Speaker of the Saskatchewan Legislative Assembly from 1905 to 1908 after the province was formed. Previous to this, Honourable William Eakin was the Speaker of the Legislative Assembly of the North-West Territories from 1899 to 1902. His chair, also probably crafted by John McGuirl, is in the Legion Hall at Saltcoats.[21]

As well, "the chair used during the last sessions of Territorial Legisla-ture occupied by Honourable A. B. Gillis of Whitewood, speaker of the assembly from 1903 to 1905" is located in the reading room of the library in the leg-islative building in Regina (see photo on page 5). There is sufficient reason to believe McGuirl also had a hand in its construction.[22] In addition, McGuirl probably made the chair of the first Speaker of the legislative assembly of the Territories, Herbert Charles Wilson, M.D. of Edmonton, who resided from 1888 to 1891. It now sits in Government House in Edmonton.

At least, in all cases of the Speaker's chairs, the dates fit with the requests from the government for desks that McGuirl certainly received. The designs of the chairs are also of a similar nature to one another, and unique to McGuirl's style in other pieces of furniture that are definitely known to be his, such as the chairs found in the Moosomin Masonic Lodge. According to notes made by Bert McKay, "McGuirl also made other handsome furni-ture for the Legislature, as well as council chambers..."[23] and it seems quite likely speaker's chairs were among the items he designed.

Exterior & interior (below) of St. Alban's Anglican Church, Moosomin, totally built by McGuirl

Most definitely McGuirl, manufactured Lieutenant-Governor Edgar Dewdney's unique desk, when the government dignitary was equipping his chambers in Regina for meetings of the North-West Council. It bore a hand-carved Royal Coat of Arms, and the appropriate words: "Parva sub Ingenti." McGuirl had sent him a sample of his best desk, which was well received by its beneficiary, and on September 3, 1885, McGuirl received an order for twenty-two more desks and a note: "The specimen sent to His Honor proved satisfactory in every respect."[24]

Bishops Chair, St. Alban's Anglican Church

Consequently, McGuirl shipped twenty-three desks to Regina for the Council Chamber in October, 1885, six desks of the same pattern in 1888, and two more in 1891. For the first batch he charged $10.60 each and for the ones in 1888 only $9.83.[25] It's not clear if he continued to manufacture further desks when the assembly was increased to thirty-four members in 1902, and under the province to forty-one members in 1908.[26] However, in June of 1911, when the Assembly was about to move to the present legislative building where new furniture had been installed, the former desks were shipped as gifts to the men using them at the time.[27] Perhaps one of McGuirl's more resourceful ventures occurred in 1886 when his factory created a new type of school desk.

"The McGuirl desk is novel in design, of wonderful strength and durability, combining all the improvements of patent desks, and yet without patent and without an equal. It is made entirely of the best seasoned wood and wrought iron, no cast being used. The manufacturer, having special facilities for the production of these articles, is able to sell them at a figure that defies competition in the eastern markets, and this recommends itself to every school board in the West."[28]

This undertaking probably resulted in McGuirl receiving the contract that year for supplying the seating and furniture for Moosomin's first two-storey school, Academy Hall. The building was a combination elementary, high school and Normal school. Also that same year McGuirl provided the Cecil Hotel of Moose Jaw with "one of the finest solid quartered-oak office counters in the West.... [He] also supplied doors, windows, and fine furnishings."[29] As well, in 1892 McGuirl turned out some handsome office fittings for the local Union Bank, and subsequently took a contract to supply quality furniture for all the new branches of the Union Bank in the west.[30]

Life for McGuirl was good, and his furniture factory business was expanding and doing well. In May of 1888 one of the local newspapers reported John McGuirl erecting a large two-storey building for his lumber business on South Street.[31] A week later, the paper states that McGuirl's "warehouse and mattress factory was nearly complete, and that he was expecting the largest and best assortment to arrive in Assiniboia East. With his own manufacturing facilities he will be enabled to sell goods at the right price, at last."[32] Three years later, also in May, a local news item mentions that McGuirl had completed the conversion of his plant to steam power. In August of the next year it was reported that McGuirl was "adding to his premises, the foundation for the shop being 24 feet by 40 feet, and for the engine room and drying kiln, 14 feet by 80 feet." Obviously his business was successful and seemed to increase each year.

However, tragedy struck on May 17, 1898, when a fire started in the engine room of the plant, "and made such rapid headway that an in an incredibly short time the whole inside of the factory was filled with flame and smoke." McGuirl's son Charlie, "in charge of the engine, was firing up with shavings and cuttings from the floor, where the planer and other machinery were placed, when a puff of flames burst out through the fire-grate and ignited the rest of the shavings placed in front of the engine." This spread so quickly nothing was saved in the main building. Only a small shed of cabinet material nearby remained unscathed. The $500 worth of material had been saved with great difficulty.

There was no insurance of any kind, and the damage resulted in a $5,000 loss. However, McGuirl managed to build a factory twice as big, fully powered by steam. Thus he was able to re-open on September 13 in 1898 under the title "McGuirl and Barclay."[33] Almost immediately, they were hired to erect a 16 foot farm windmill which was to power one of the first grain crushers in the west.[34]

Not only a furniture craftsman and a general contractor, McGuirl was a forerunner in innovation and ingenuity when it came to working with wood. His work was in demand throughout the prairies, and indeed he received orders for house furnishings in the East as well.[35] In time the Moose Jaw and Oxbow Anglican Churches[36] were fully furnished by the Moosomin Planing Mill, and Christ Church of Wapella received an oak chair, a back organ stool and two altar chairs made of solid oak in 1903.[37]

About 1910, the new Church of England in Moose Jaw also ordered a quarter-cut pulpit. "The carvings, and in fact all of the work, on this piece is perfect, and when finished it will be impossible to find a nail mark anywhere."[38]

Chiefly McGuirl crafted his articles using peg and glue construction. In the case of some artifacts, such as the backs of chairs, he would level off an area and then create a pebbled effect. The furniture, made in the main from old English or quarter-cut oak, was richly finished in 19th century Gothic and Corinthian styles,[39] many of which were ornately decorated with hand-carvings.

Pews made by McGuirl in Oxbow Anglican Church

Sample of carved columns in Masonic Lodge, Moosomin

In order to identify McGuirl's work, many of his furniture pieces often had a silver or brass plate attached, upon which was engraved "Manufactured by John McGuirl, Moosomin, Sask." Others had similarly worded labels, but not everything that came from McGuirl's factory was designated as such, and now his pieces are sometimes difficult to distinguish or authenticate with any definite accuracy. On the other hand, there were few other woodworkers of his skill, doing similar types of work to such a large degree during that time frame.

For sure, McGuirl's work was recognized for his expert craftsmanship by his own community. In 1903 the *Moosomin World-Spectator* said, "It is a great credit to Moosomin to have a local firm that can turn out such excellent work, and it is a source of great satisfaction to know that work of such high class can be created right here in our town, without having to send to outside points for it." McGuirl indeed, had every right to be proud of his accomplishments.

There is every indication that he took his woodworking business seriously, but there was another side to the man. It seems besides, being "an artist and gifted raconteur, McGuirl was also noted for something in a different field...yodelling. He is reported appearing at various concerts to entertain with this then-new form of art, long before Hollywood discovered gold in yodelling cowboys."[40]

McGuirl also had other talents and pursuits, which ironically he could relate back to his woodworking. In fact, this interest produced one of the most ingenious objects to come out of McGuirl's factory—hockey sticks. These were shipped all over the West. McGuirl's son Jim was reputedly one of the better players of his day, and the hockey sticks for his team were made in the McGuirl factory, just 50 feet from the rink.[41]

In fact, "reports indicate that Jim and the other young hockey players spent many hours in the evenings [after hours], making their own hockey sticks in the McGuirl plant. As the puck in those days was three layers of oval leather, nailed together, the sticks had to be strong to say the least." However, "there was plenty of steam to put just the right curve in those rather crude, but durable hockey sticks. Some were even made from willow with the root left on to form the blade."[42]

The rink itself seems to have been instigated by McGuirl, as well. He's quoted in 1884 in the November 20th issue of *The Courier,* then Moosomin's newest paper, as saying he was going to open a skating rink in the town. Up until that time, there was only skating by lantern light on Moosomin Lake.

With the rink in place and the hockey sticks being made right next door, it's not surprising that Moosomin has been called the "birthplace of hockey in Saskatchewan." Records show that hockey was well-organized in Moosomin before it was played any other place in the North-West Territory, thanks perhaps to John McGuirl.[43]

There is little doubt that John McGuirl was a forerunner in his craft, and that his influence is in evidence throughout the province, particularly in the eastern portion. According to McKay's article in 1974 "a few old houses in eastern Saskatchewan still feature the ornate and solid banister work in their front stairs, and a number of handsome church pulpits are still in use, with the McGuirl silver or brass plate still in place underneath."[44]

The popularity of his furniture seems to have extended to most towns along the main line of the CPR, which was the only line for many of the early years that the Moosomin Planing Mill was in operation. Many towns had some of McGuirl's work in one or more places.[45]

"The fine products of Moosomin Planing Mill continued to be in demand across the West until 1912 when the plant was closed by death of the owner."[46] John McGuirl died suddenly on January 4, 1913. By then his reputation for "handsome," "neat and substantial work," and "appealing and durable articles of handicraft" was well-established. Today McGuirl's work stands solidly as evidence of his incredible ability and craftsmanship. He will be remembered as "one of the most highly skilled workmen in the West," and a master furniture maker.[47]

ENDNOTES

1. He died January 4, 1913 and is buried in the Old Anglican Church cemetery. Information from the headstone, and other records.

2. It was known that McGuirl was in Merrickville in 1871, according to the article "McGuirl family first pioneer group," in *The Moosomin World-Spectator,* Golden Jubilee Issue, June 22, 1955.

3. Ibid. Also of note, McGuirl's oldest son, James Patrick was a member of the South African Constabulary in active service during the Boer War.

4. The family arrived in April of 1883, according to a death notice in *The Moosomin World-Spectator.*

5. From *The Moosomin World-Spectator,* Golden Jubilee Issue, June 22, 1955.

6. The land location was SW 1/4 of 32-13-30. He applied for this in September of 1882, and received the patent in 1893. This information is gleaned from the Moosomin History Book; *Moosomin—Century One—Town and Country,* p. 736.

7. She was born at Smith Falls, Ontario on August 12 in 1858, according to the *Statistical Data on the McGuirl Family of Moosomin, Saskatchewan, Canada,* prepared by Otto H. Schoenberger of Moosomin, Executor of the Estate of the Late Minnie E. McGuirl of Moosomin, Sask., Canada, March 29, 1963, as noted in the family bible. She died February 7, 1935 at Long Beach, California, where she had resided since 1920,★ according to the death notice in *The Moosomin World-Spectator,* February, 1935. ★Another issue of this newspaper, the Golden Jubilee Issue, June 22, 1955, suggests she left in 1919.

8. According to the Moosomin History Book, p. 736. Her birth date was Sept. 22, 1883, according to the family bible.

9. Sarah (also known as Mida) died in an accident while visiting friends at Fleming on June 5, 1888.

10. This was Miles Edwin McGuirl.

11. From *The Moosomin World-Spectator,* Golden Jubilee Issue, June 22, 1955. Date of actual construction is unknown.

12. It's not clear exactly when the McGuirls moved into the town or when he sold his land, but according to homestead maps he still owned the land in 1905, although he was already well established in the town of Moosomin with a flourishing business.

13. Bert McKay's article, "Moosomin mill outfitted west with desks," in the *Brandon Sun,* date unknown.

14.. His son James, eventually took over the funeral parlour.

15. *The Church of St. Alban,* Moosomin, "A Brief History."

16. Taken from *The First Hundred Years,* the history of St. Alban's Anglican Church. The Young People's Guild purchased the chair in memory of the late Bishop Burn.

17. From *The Moosomin World-Spectator.*

18. From the Golden Jubilee issue of *The Moosomin World-Spectator,* June 22, 1955. McGuirl was a member of the Town council when he died in 1913.

19. Obituary in *The Moosomin World-Spectator,* ca. Feb. 12, 1935. She was buried at Long Beach, California where she had been residing since approximately 1920. She passed away on Thursday, February 7, 1935 at the age of 77.

20. James eventually took over his father's business.

21. This information was derived from the *Saltcoats History Book:* 1982.

22. Information from *Sentinel of the Prairies: the Saskatchewan Legislative Building,* by Gordon Barnhart, [n.d.]

23. From an article in the *Leader-Post,* January 3, 1974, written by Bert McKay of Moosomin, who did extensive research into McGuirl's work. Bert McKay is now deceased, but a record of his files is available.

24. Ibid.

25. Ibid.

26. According to a letter to Bert McKay, from Allan R. Turner, Provincial Archivist, November 29, 1973.

27. The whereabouts of the majority of these desks is unknown.

28. From the Moosomin *Courier,* March 11, 1886.

29. McKay's article.

30. Local news items recorded in various newspapers.

31. In notes derived from the two local newspapers. He apparently built right "next door to Captain Harris."

32. Ibid. May 10th issue.

33. Although there is not evidence of such, perhaps this indicates that McGuirl went into partnership with someone.

34. Referred to in McKay's article. Also mentioned in the Moosomin *Courier,* May 19, 1898, which notes that the windmill belonged to W. M. Hill, who lived near the Pipestone Valley. The windmill was a Fairbanks Morse product.

35. From notes taken from the sixth issue of the new Moosomin paper, the *Courier,* on November 13, 1884.

36. The Oxbow Anglican Church had a number of oak pews, the pulpit, a reading desk and an altar table made by McGuirl.

37. Newspaper notation, May 23, 1903.

38. *The Moosomin World-Spectator,* 1910.

39. McKay article in the *Leader-Post,* Dec. 16, 1974.

40. McKay article, the *Brandon Sun.*

41. From Bert McKay's *Notes on John McGuirl and the Moosomin Planing Mill, May 23, 1903.*

42. Ibid, taken from the *Moosomin World-Spectator,* 1910.

43. Organized hockey, mainly between Moosomin and teams in Manitoba, was played in Moosomin well before the game was enjoyed in points west such as Indian Head, Regina, and Moose Jaw, according to Bert McKay.

44. The article appeared in *The Leader-Post,* Regina, Monday, December 16, 1974.

45. According to McKay's article.

46. Bert McKay's article in *The Leader-Post,* Regina, Monday, December 16, 1974.

47. John McGuirl's son James took over the business, but eventually he whittled it down to just running the funeral parlour.

OLAF (OLE) LINUS PEARSON
(1868-1961)

WITHOUT A DOUBT, OLAF LINUS PEARSON WAS THE most ingenious and prolific woodworker to emerge in Saskatchewan during the early 1900s. An artist whose medium happened to be wood, his productive period spanned more than seventy years. During that time Pearson created hundreds of distinctive artifacts and pieces of furniture. Even his tools were crafted with incredible detail and precision. Anything that could be constructed of wood he produced, making use of the large variety of native woods available. In addition, Pearson hand-carved almost every piece he made, often adding hidden drawers and secret compartments as a challenge to unsuspecting admirers of his work.

Although somewhat of an eccentric, Pearson was an extraordinary craftsman, who cared deeply for his chosen profession. This passion and the opportunity to make a better living at woodworking influenced Pearson in his decision to emigrate from Sweden to Canada in 1894. Certainly, farming did not lure him.

Even though he eventually bought a quarter section of land seven

Pearson family portrait

miles east of Broadview, the romantic notion of tilling the rich virgin soil and producing golden fields of grain under wide azure prairie skies failed to arouse 26-year-old Ole Pearson to action. He never farmed the land to any great extent. Instead, he left the farm management to the capable hands of his young nephew Andrew Anderson, who came to live with the Pearsons when the boy's family moved to B.C. Ole Pearson's every intention was to concentrate on carpentry and woodworking in his new adopted country.

Born on Nov. 26, 1868, to Ingeborg and Per Rask, he was christened Olaf Linus Rask, but shed his last name and his homeland upon immigrating to Canada. Name changes were a common Swedish practice, and as the "son of Per," his name easily transformed to Person, later Anglicized to Pearson.[1] Although little is known about Pearson's early life, he was relatively well-educated and he became a carpenter by trade. This was not surprising—woodworking was one of Sweden's most important industries.[2]

Raised in Jamtland County,[3] a central inland area of Sweden bordering Norway high in the Kjolen Mountains, Pearson was familiar with the properties of spruce and Scotch pine that covered much of the region. He knew the traits of the stunted birch and willow trees found in a zone of the moorlands below, and he sometimes worked with the oak and beech that dominated the lowlands to the south.[4] Pearson expected plenty of similar woods in Canada. Other factors about immigrating, like the weather, seemed inconsequential to him. As Pearson soon found out, the cold and the wind could be just as severe in winter on the Canadian prairies as they had been in Sweden.

Pearson, and later his parents and several siblings, were only a few of the one million immigrants who came to Canada from the Scandinavian countries or North America during the early settlement years around the turn of the century.[5] Those that came to the Saskatchewan prairies settled mostly in the eastern region of the province. The largest population swell was around Stockholm, but Percival was also a thriving Swedish community in Pearson's day.[6]

Accessibly situated between Broadview and Whitewood along the CPR line, settlers appeared on the Percival horizon as plentiful as dandelions in the spring. Named after "members of a well known English family, who settled there in the early days,"[7] Percival suited Pearson in several ways. True, the area lacked any resemblance to the forested mountain country he had come from, nor did it have abundant lakes, but there was

Pearson home, originally made of logs

Pearson workshop

enough water around for Pearson to indulge in an occasional fishing trip. He also seemed satisfied with the variety of local woods in the nearby Pipestone Valley.

When he first arrived in the area, Pearson worked for the CPR out of Broadview as a section man, keeping the miles of track shovelled clear of snow in the winter and in good repair all year round.

"Many Swedish men were hired and had the advantage of having worked on railroads in their homeland. They made $1.40 per day and paid $4.00 per week for their board," according to the Broadview History Book.[8] Whether or not Pearson had any previous railroad experience is not known, but this was a typical occupation at the time.

The job was not easy, particularly in winter where the snow blew at will over the vast expanse of prairie. The importance of these jobs became even more apparent when the Silk Trains with their precious cargoes worth ten million dollars sped across the continent from Vancouver to New York. Nothing and no one had precedence over these highballing rollers. Even the future King Edward VIII's train was placed in a siding in December of 1919 to allow a "Silker" to keep to its precarious timetable.[9] "God help the railroader who delayed a Silker," Pearson heard often enough, even after he had quit working for the railroad.[10]

Lathe made by Pearson   Planes, carved box and hook

Pearson's talents as a carpenter were soon in demand building homes for the influx of settlers, and by 1900 he had purchased his "farm."[11] This was also the same year he married Martha Olson, a young enthusiastic girl from Broadview, with sparkling brown eyes and a disposition to match. She pitched right in, helping to build their spacious log home, which is still in good condition and occupied today.

From time to time, Pearson was hired for contracting jobs. He, along with his nephew, constructed the Bethel Church at Oakshela,[12] and he also built some of the pews still in use today at Grace Canadian Lutheran Church in Broadview.[13] His talents always seemed to be in demand.

Between carpentry jobs, Pearson built himself a workshop on the farm. Here he constructed a myriad of built-in shelves and tiny intricate cupboards on every wall. This was his haven, where he spent endless hours creating a variety of hand-crafted pieces and tools. Even years later, when he finally bought a gas-powered motor he preferred to work by hand. The engine sat idle and power tools never entered his shop.[14]

Word of Pearson's skill and the quality of his work spread like a brush fire on a windy day. Incredibly patient, Pearson ensured every tiny piece of wood fit precisely, and his designs were all original. Some of his favourites were the curved-top boxes that he hand-engraved from burls and sometimes dyed with coloured wax. Pearson finished them with unique hinges and clasps often in the shape of animals or birds that he also made, fashioning them from solder, brass, tin or sometimes copper, all using his own designs.

Carved bit boxes   Pearson desk with secret compartments

His imagination never ceased to amaze people. He delighted in hiding secret drawers and compartments in many of his ornate boxes and desks. Usually Pearson had to show people where they were located. Of particular fascination was a life-like, duck-shaped box with drawers in the chest and the butt end, and hinged ones on either side that looked like the wings in flight when opened. Sometimes he took many days to finish one meticulous object.

Every knife, wood plane or tool Pearson owned, he made, including any metal parts. But none were simple. Each was a highly imaginative

Carved chisel box

Specially designed plane

piece of artistry. Almost every tool had some sort of inlay or carving, whether Pearson made it from one block of wood or added a burl. And every file and drill bit had its own precisely fitting storage box with a sliding top and dividers inside. Many toolboxes had several levels and intriguing doors, drawers and removable trays. Even his lathe, which he built entirely from scraps, showed his expertise.

Methodical and patient, Pearson's early work was mainly done in pine, which he probably bought through Fredlund's Lumber Yard and Hardware store in Percival.[15] For his later items, he utilized birch and maple, both accessible in the nearby valley. All his products could be ordered or were available from those he had on hand. They were easily identified—Pearson liked to engrave his initials prominently on his work. Sometimes his pieces were also dated.

Many of Pearson's items that still exist today are smaller, but he made numerous dressers and desks with a variety of decorative touches from inlays and templated-carvings to added mouldings. One of his unique pieces was a doghouse for his own small mutt that he acquired in later years. Pearson replicated a real gable-roofed house in every detail, complete with shingles, chimney and door latches. Then he carved the dog's face on the roof.

Doghouse for Pearson's small dog
(Side views and top view)

A cabinetmaker by trade, Pearson also loved the challenge of unusual requests, like wool carders, rope makers, document boxes, and grave markers. He utilized every scrap of wood he could, wasting nothing. Whether he used layers, mouldings or fashioned his own templates, the quality of his work spoke for itself. His customers were always gratified by his craftsmanship and his inventiveness.

No request was declined if he felt it could be done, including a bloodletting device for his wife. Martha suffered from high blood pressure as she aged and at that time there were no medicines available. Pearson fashioned a small jackknife-like instrument with a hooked blade, which sprang out and cut open a vein. Martha let the blood flow until she felt the pressure subside, then she secured the wound and replaced the tool into a kitchen drawer until the next time it was needed.[16]

Fancy cupboard

A shy man by nature, Pearson's reservations were forgotten as he regaled his well-known acquaintances and neighbours with anecdotes while he worked in the comfort of his shop. The Pearsons, with their two daughters, Ingeborg and Martha, were a popular family and often had visitors, sometimes much to Ole's annoyance.

"I'll be in right away. I just have a little to finish," he'd say and disappear back into his shop. At times he just didn't make an appearance until the company was ready to leave, so caught up was he in his work. At every opportunity he worked with his wood projects, often late into the night. Sometimes he needed to be rejuvenated or to think a new design through, and that's when he escaped to other favourite diversions, such as fishing or attending to his car.

Pearson always owned a nice-looking car in the later years, and jealously guarded the appearance and condition of it. Meticulous as always, he gave it frequent washings and polishings, never driving it any more often than was warranted.[17] A proficient violinist, he played for relaxation only, and without an audience. On the odd occasion he slipped away to fish, sitting patiently for hours on the banks of the nearby Qu'Appelle River.[18] But his woodworking remained his main reason for existence.

He constantly made furniture and gadgets for his family, including a two-wheeled child's cart and pull-out bed for his grandson, Lloyd.

Child's wagon

Bed-couch

Fashioned more like an eastern European article with its straw mattress, it doubled as a bench during the day.

"He made the bed for me over sixty years ago. I slept in it for a good many years," said Lloyd, who sometimes cranked his grandfather's lathe. "He also made Grandma these rolling pins out of birch. They're for making 'thin bread.'"

As the years rolled by Pearson became more eccentric and obsessed with chicken images. They appeared everywhere: in the shape of hinges, drawn onto the sides of bowls and carved on handles of his wood planes. Even the door latch on his outhouse was fashioned in the shape of a chicken with the beak serving as the hook.[19]

Mac Provich, an avid collector and admirer of Pearson's work, wrote from Churchbridge, "He worked continually even into advanced age with firm control of his tools and no apparent reduction of his imagination to produce items pleasing to the eye."

Until Pearson died in 1961, at the age of 92, he was still active with his woodwork pursuits, and when a year later an auction sale was held on his farm, hundreds of pieces of his woodwork were sold. His daughters had predeceased him, and other family members kept very little. Most went to private collectors who recognized the quality of his work, his value as an artist and perhaps the genius of the man.

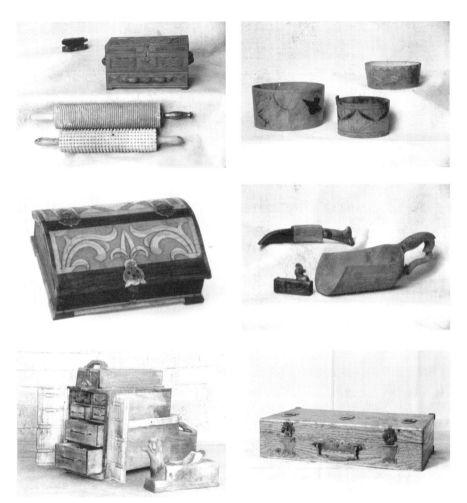

Household items including a bloodletting devise (top left photo, top left-hand corner), rolling pins for making lefsa, flour scoops, knives, bowls (note chicken designs), decorative boxes, a small plane, unfinished multi-drawer box, and wooden box (note hand made clasps and handles).

ENDNOTES
_____

1. According to conversations with Lloyd Pearson.

2. Refsal, Harley. *Woodcarving in the Scandinavian Style.* New York: Sterling Publishing, Co. Inc., 1992. P. 15. Also: Golden Press Inc. *Golden Home Encyclopedia,* "Sweden" (New York: Golden Press Inc, 1961) p. 2477.

3. Mac Provich notes.

4. Ibid.

5. Times Books Ltd. *The Times Atlas of World History* (London: Fitzhenry & Whiteside Limited, 1979), pp. 208-209.

6. Richards, J. H. & Fung, K. I., Editors, *Atlas of Saskatchewan,* (Saskatoon: Modern Press, 1969), p. 13.

   Note: Besides Percival and Stockholm, there were also Swedish settlements at Glen Mary in the north, the Outlook area, and an area between Foam Lake and Sheho.

7. Broadview Pioneer History Society, *Story of Broadview and Area: Centennial Tribute, Oakshela, Broadview, Percival, 1882-1982,* (Altona, Manitoba: Friesen Printers, 1982), p. 109.

   "It was a member of this family, Spencer Percival, who while prime minister of Britain (1809-1912) was assassinated by a bankrupt broker, John Bellingham."

8. Ibid, p. 11

9. Hall, Trevor. *Royal Canada,* (Godalming, Surrey, England: Archive Publishing, a subsidiary of Colour Library Books Ltd., 1989.)

   The Broadview History Book also makes note of this incident, however the name of the royal person they cited was incorrect.

10. Broadview Pioneer Society, *Story of Broadview and Area: Centennial Tribute, Oakshela, Broadview, Percival, 1882-1982,* (Altona, Manitoba: Friesen Printers, 1982), p. 25.

11. Interview with Lloyd Pearson, grandson. Land location: SE¼ 34-16-4 W2.

12. Broadview Pioneer Society, *Story of Broadview and Area: Centennial Tribute, Oakshela, Broadview, Percival, 1882-1982,* (Altona, Manitoba: Friesen Printers, 1982), p 159.

13. Ibid, p. 119.

14. According to grandson, Lloyd Pearson.

15. Living along the rail line, Pearson was able to have wood brought in, which was probably sold through this store, as it was the only one in the area.

16. Conversations with grandson, Lloyd Pearson.

17. Conversations and letters from Mac Provich.

18. From conversations and letters with Lloyd Pearson.

19. Although the outhouse remains, an ardent admirer removed the latch.

JOACHIM PILON
(1864-1962)

A CABINETMAKER KNOWN FOR HIS INNOVATIVENESS AND diamond willow artifacts, Joachim Pilon's daring and adventurous spirit was first revealed when he took up the challenge as a *voyageur du bois* in the early 1880s. Wearing a colourful woven sash, a *ceintures flechées,*[1] Pilon proudly rode the logs down the demanding rivers in the Laurentian area of Quebec. An accident several years later, when he split his foot with an axe, changed the course of his life.

By the time Joachim was born on April 19, 1864, the Pilon family already had been established in Canada for at least seven generations.[2] Although it's not conclusive that they came from Brittany, it is believed the Pilons came from somewhere in France.[3] The first Pilon, Antoine, arrived in Montreal in 1688, where he married a year later. Each successive generation seems to have remained in the surrounding vicinity.

Joachim's stern parents, Joseph Pilon and Sophie Miron, lived in a two-storey house in the town of St. Jerome approximately fifty kilometres northeast of Montreal.[4] Later they moved to La Conception, where today there is a street named after this Pilon family which passes over the river where the sawmill Joseph operated once stood on its bank.[5] Their local church still rests on the other side, where Joachim's grandfather Amble is buried in the nearby churchyard.

The seventh child of eleven, Joachim struggled not to be just one of a large family, but to make an important mark with his life. Possibilities for his formal education were limited, and according to family sources he probably went only to the third grade, if at all.[6] Since his father was in the logging business, it seemed natural that Joachim would also find interest in aspects of the trade. By the time he married Clara Villeneuve in 1882, he was already a *coureur de bois,* and they began living at La Conception, about one hundred and fifteen kilometres straight north of Montreal.[7] Here their three eldest children were born, one dying at the age of three.

Joachim's accident occurred while he was logging in the woods, causing him to seek his fortune elsewhere. He uprooted his family and moved to Chicago in 1888, where he found work as a carpenter's helper. By 1892, Joachim and Clara had six children, most of whom didn't know any of their relatives in Quebec, so the family decided to return to La Conception to become reacquainted. Considered to be the black sheep of the family because he had moved away, Joachim was treated coolly by his mother. On the first day of his return, she sat on the balcony of her house and watched him walk by without speaking or acknowledging him.

Pilon's two-story shop. Note the fire wagon on sleighs, which was later converted with wheels and is still used today in parades

Conditions gradually improved with his extended family when his mother thawed towards him, but other problems gnawed at him. Although Pilon found some work at various jobs to earn his living, he realized logging was what he knew best in the area. However, this occupation was something he no longer could or wanted to do. Dissatisfied with his life, by 1900 Pilon's feet tingled to move on again, and he returned to Chicago where working with wood drew him.

He applied with the Pullman Car Company, indicating on his application that he was a qualified carpenter, even though he had no experience in house construction. The company gave him some men and a set of plans, directing him to assemble one of the company houses being built for the workers. If he could do this satisfactorily, they would hire him to continue building houses. Astutely, Pilon spent his evenings inspecting another house being built, one where the construction was two or three days in advance of his own. He would copy the work the next day. In this fashion, he completed three or four houses, often discovering mistakes made by others, which enabled him to improve the quality of his own work.

The company soon recognized his efforts, and made Pilon an inspector in the factory where the Pullman Cars were being built. At that time the cars were all made of wood. The large variety of solid woods and the choice kinds of veneers inspired Pilon. He began collecting the scraps and piecing them together to fashion checkerboard tables and corner cupboards in his off hours. Some of these items are still in existence today, including one large checkerboard table, which folds when not in use, and has hidden drawers for storing the checkers.

Pilon remained happily in the factory for several years, pursuing his woodworking pastimes. He enjoyed the occasional bit of excitement, like the time he and his fellow workers were given a half-day off to witness the finale of the race between Wilbur Wright's plane and a steam locomotive. Life in Chicago seemed to suit the whole family; however several years later, the Pilons were dismayed when the Pullman Company switched to making their cars out of steel. The increased loudness of the riveting noises bothered Pilon's ears, and itchy feet once again claimed him in 1911.

Pilon building construction

This time his adventurous spirit called him to the west. Edmonton was near the end of the railroad and this seemed as good a place as any for the Pilons to relocate. Joachim took his eldest son Edmond with him by rail via Winnipeg. As they travelled, they made an assessment of each town until they reached Edmonton. Once there, they realized that city wasn't the place for them, and they backtracked to have another look at Melville. Soon afterwards the whole family, by now including nine children, packed and moved into the town.[8]

The four oldest children returned to Chicago a short time later, where they made their homes and raised their offspring. The remainder stayed in Melville, and an older brother of Joachim's, Napoleon, settled nearby in Lebret with his family.[9]

Once in Melville, Pilon bought a blacksmith shop, which was situated on 3rd Avenue and Saskatchewan St. When the demand for sleighs, cutters, carriages and wagons of all kinds increased, he built a two-storey building around his shop.[10] The wagon wheels and ironworks were formed on the main floor, with the wood finishing and painting completed on the second. The units were raised and lowered from one floor to the other by a series of blocks and tackles. One of these items crafted by Pilon was a fire wagon, which today is preserved in the Melville fire hall for use in local parades.

Eventually motorized vehicles appeared on the scene and the need for carriage and wagon products

Pilon tools

died. Pilon, along with his son, Noel Joseph, turned instead to house building at which he seemed to excel. Even the challenge of building a circular staircase without any previous experience, or knowledge of geometry, proved not to be an obstacle for Pilon. Besides building numerous single and duplex houses in Melville, Pilon also constructed smaller items like the windows in the local Catholic Church.[11] During the thirties when income was scarce, he made caskets in order to put food on the table.[12]

Most of Pilon's tools were hand-made, and he took pride in his work. He firmly believed, and often repeated to family and co-workers that, "If a job was worth doing, it was worth doing well."[13] Each of his artifacts portrays this belief.

Pilon's talents were many. Although almost totally self-taught, his cabinets were exquisitely executed. Curved designs were featured in corner bookshelves, and china cabinets, all intricately fitted and finished. He also made mirrors, doll cupboards, footstools, board games, dressers, beds, rocking chairs, and miniature replicas of furniture.

Although he never deliberately imported any woods, he was able to secure several different kinds from the local lumberyard. Usually, however, he used whatever people brought to him, or whatever was available locally. Many of his pieces were made from oak, maple, fir, and pine.

Then Pilon discovered the beauty of diamond willow.[14] Before long he was turning out floor lamps, table lamps, table legs and walking canes. One particularly exquisite piece features a hand-carved tulip lampshade made from one piece of wood and a diamond willow stand that supports a small checkerboard table with hidden side drawers.

Lamp

Checkerboard table and lamp

Although Pilon found some diamond willow locally, mostly he secured it from the Lebret and Spy Hill areas in Saskatchewan, and the St. Lazare region of Manitoba. His son Don, who worked on the railroad, would bring the diamond willow back to him, then Pilon would let it dry and age before stripping the bark. Once this was done, and the natural diamond shapes revealed, he would hand carve the remainder of the limb, creating a piece suitable for one of his many ongoing projects. With painstaking precision and loving care, he turned gnarled and knotty boughs into works of art.

A warm, gentle man, Joachim Pilon loved his family, especially children, equally as much as his woodworking. At Christmas time, he'd make small replicas of furniture, a china cabinet or dresser, for each of his children, then allow them the pleasure of finding the pieces and claiming one gift as their own. As the years passed and his family grew, his grandchildren and great-grandchildren always seemed drawn to this quiet, patient man.

Known as a man who never intentionally hurt anyone in his life, Pilon exuded kindness. Although he was more comfortable speaking the French he grew up learning, he never spoke it in front of someone

Child's toy dresser

Bookcase

without the courtesy of a translation. He learned English on his own, and in his later years, his keen interest in the world around him, led him to read many articles of interest in the *Encyclopedia Britannica.*[15]

When he was about 78 years old, he built his last duplex home,[16] and then began constructing violins in his spare time. He created seven of them for others, and spent many leisure hours learning to play his own violin. Although he held a deep appreciation for vegetable and flower gardening, he left this pastime for the capable hands of his wife.

Clara was the kind of woman who took everything in stride. An intelligent, quiet woman, she was a dedicated homemaker who loved cooking and caring for their large family. Although strict, she was generous and kind, supporting her husband's ventures throughout their years together.

Pilon was hardly ever sick in his life; yet as he aged, his movement became limited, and he often enjoyed sitting at the front window in his house, watching people go by. A very particular man, he was never seen without a tie, even when he was at home.[17]

Violin

Child's china cabinet, which stands approx. 30" high

Corner cupboard

Fire wagon used in parades today.

He died a month before his ninety-ninth birthday on March 27, 1962. During his life, he had not been afraid of adventure, of learning, of taking risks, or of performing his tasks to the best of his abilities. Creative and endearing to the last, even though he was a man without formal education or training, Pilon indeed left his mark in history with his exquisite pieces of woodwork.

ENDNOTES

1. A woven sash called *ceintures fléchees* worn by Métis (a meld of European and native heritage) voyageurs.

2. Any previous records were lost when the local church in La Conception burnt down.

3. According to family stories handed down to Ed and Roch Pilon, Joachim's grandsons, the Pilon's came from Brittany, although this can't be confirmed. They are quite sure the Pilon family originally came from somewhere in France, and believe that seven to nine generations have lived in Canada.

4. Taped conversation with Roch Pilon.

5. According to an interview with Roch Pilon, this sawmill was destroyed by fire some years ago.

6. From an interview with Roch Pilon. Joachim Pilon could read and write, French and English.

7. Taped conversations with Roch Pilon.

8. Joachim and Clara had five daughters: Bertha, Lea, Ida, Alma, and Diana. The first three named, lived in Canada, along with two of Joachim and Clara's sons Noel Joseph and Don. The older boys moved back to Chicago.

9. Napoleon was the sixth child of eleven.

10. Today this building is known as the Millar Apartments, but originally was referred to as the Pilon Block. (Taken from interview notes with Ed and Roch Pilon.)

11. The original Catholic Church with the window made by Pilon burned down, and was replaced by a new church and parish centre.

12. Interview with Roch Pilon.

13. Ibid.

14. Possibly in the 1940s and 50s, he worked more extensively with diamond willow.

15. His daughter Bertha, who was a teacher, gave him a set of encyclopedias, according to Roch Pilon.

16. Ed Pilon, Joachim's grandson, lives in this house today.

17. According to an interview with Ed Pilon.

CHARLES SMITH (1890-1961)
AND HAROLD COOMBS (1883-1964)

ERHAPS THE MOST INGENUOUS OF WOODWORKERS WERE
those who relied totally on their own resources, who weren't afraid
to be inventive or to express themselves. These were the ones who
became excellent scroungers, utilizing recycled products to the fullest, or
devising methods of overcoming limited building materials. Although
their work might not necessarily be considered superior in view of the
sometimes-crude construction, there was skill involved, and their creations are a valued contribution to folk art and history.

Of those who were inspired and utilized their surroundings, two perhaps stand out: Harold Coombs of Maymont, and Charles Smith of
Coderre. Both became excellent "scavengers," although Coombs might be
considered the most outrageous of the pair in terms of articles he produced. Smith, on the other hand, was diligent and pragmatic, yet managed
to create sustainable, fine items for functional home use.

CHARLES SMITH (1890-1961)

Although both men originally arrived from Great Britain, there the similarities end. Charles Smith was born in Scotland on September 5, 1890 to a shepherd's family, a pursuit he also chose to follow as he grew up.[1] He was still living with his parents, John Smith and Annie Campbell, at Newlands Cottage in the country of Dumfries, before the wanderlust spirit came over him.

Upon arriving on the prairies, Smith first settled in Regina. This was about 1912, just in time for him to experience the devastating cyclone that occurred that year.[2] In 1914 he joined the Regina Rifle Regiment, serving for four years. On his discharge, he found work for one summer in the Odessa/Kendal area, but by the fall of 1918 he settled at Coderre,[3] taking out a homestead from the dispersal of the W Bar Ranch. This was a huge company-owned ranch that consisted of thousands of acres, "stretching from the Wood River south to the U.S. border,"[4] and running from just a little farther east than Coderre, encompassing Shamrock Park, to Swift Current in the west.[5]

Once Smith had established his homestead, he married Alice Brew on September 7, 1920, in Regina. At that time Charles was a little short on cash, and his new wife had to pay for the taxi ride home.[6] Although

Smith homestead

Smith at his home.

finances didn't improve substantially, they eventually had seven children, raising them with the help of a hired woman,[7] all of them living in the old bachelor shack that Smith had first built. Of course, the tiny place had to be revamped occasionally to accommodate the increasing family.

The area the Smith's lived in was a desolate place in many ways. Essentially, the area was treeless, and not conducive to woodworkers. The rolling hills afforded some comfort, at least for range cattle, and perhaps even sheep, if Smith had been so inclined. However, he never attempted to raise them, and seems not to have known much about raising cattle, or about farming, either.

His family has said, "He was a great horseman, but he'd starve a cow. He couldn't raise a cow to save his soul."[8] Luckily he only had four cows, but he didn't have time for them, though he did have some measure of success with chickens. He loved driving his horses, however, and often kept six or eight of them on his farm. He used them for working the land, and drove them to town, tying up their tails with red ribbons and dressing them with fancy harnesses.

During the Second World War, he spent many hours travelling around the neighbourhood with his horses and cart, selling Canada Savings Bonds. This was just one of his many methods for supplementing his meagre farm income. A kind-hearted man he also donated much of his time to helping others.

Both Charles and Alice spent a number of years on the Bar Hill School Board as trustees, and after taking some training, Smith also became the local secretary for the Rural Municipality of Shamrock. As well, he served as the secretary for the school board, and with the Canadian Legion Local 22 B.E.S.L. for many years.[9]

Smith mitt box

Smith's connection with the legion enabled him in his woodworking pursuits, and provided a great resource for his ingenuity. He was the one that distributed the food to surrounding families, so he had access to the main packing boxes from which he secured much of his building material. These were usually apple and cheese boxes, but Smith found them serviceable for the items he needed to make.

Although he didn't have the opportunity to become very well educated, and never had any special training in woodworking, Smith managed to grasp the essentials, and then learned to improvise and create solid, fine pieces. He made chests, cupboards and sewing baskets, dish cabinets, corner shelves, knick-knack shelves, bedroom wall cabinets, picture frames, handkerchief boxes, sewing boxes, planters, a large trunk, a bench, a kitchen stool, and even a ship carved out of a cedar post.

He easily made a bench used for storing mitts and toques from apple boxes. The label is still attached on the inside to prove it.[10] Items like these were sometimes a challenge to make, because he had to work with three different thicknesses of wood—all that was available to him. The cheese containers were tall and circular, and usually held several rounds of cheese. They were perfect for sewing materials that doubled as seats with the storage area neatly tucked away inside.

Smith often enhanced his artifacts with fretwork while sitting at the kitchen table. Not all of his pieces were so adorned. Ones like sewing boxes and handkerchief boxes, were further trimmed with a cloth lining, supported by another thin layer of wood, which created a favourable effect. He also made watch charm chains out of leather, braiding three strips from the back of an old mitt. He was never one to waste anything.

Smith fretwork sewing box

While farming took precedence, Smith often pursued his woodworking during the winter months, perhaps thinking and planning the items he'd make as he sowed and harvested his crops during the summer. Smith salvaged any bits of building material, and had a knack of improvising with the most limited of materials. It is doubtful that he ever purchased much in the way of lumber, as he simply didn't have any money to do so, like so many during the tough times of the Great Depression.

Although he began doing his woodwork in the 1920s, the majority of his work was done in the following decade. However, by 1938 he had to quit any kind of hand work because of his crippling arthritis. He also had an enlarged heart, and for the last thirty years of his life, he was mostly bedridden.

He continued to be a cheerful person, nevertheless, and was known for his wonderful storytelling, taken from incidents in his personal life. He did as much as he could from home, keeping record and accounting books and such, and their home was always full of company. Although a true Scotsman, strict with his children, Smith was a giving man too, and helped wherever he could. He built many items for others throughout his life, never charging for anything.

Smith collection of cupboards, sewing boxes and mirrors.

Smith frame

During the Second World War he garnered the help of his family to send a draft for a carton of cigarettes every two weeks to the local forces of men and women overseas, and he distributed the old clothes and army surplus to needy families in the area. Hardly able to manoeuvre physically in his later years, Smith and his wife moved to Moose Jaw in 1959, with Charles passing away on July 4, 1961. Alice followed twenty-five years later.[11]

Smith's woodwork pieces are still as solid and cherished as they were fifty years earlier, a lasting reminder of improvisation and fortitude, on the part of a man who had very little in many ways for most of his life. His endurance and ingenuity can be found in his work, fine examples of the resourcefulness needed in the early pioneering years. There were others who had equally difficult lives, and those who persevered, but none quite to the extent that Smith had with all his drawbacks.

HAROLD COOMBS (1883-1964)

Men like Harold Coombs, though, managed to survive by touching a deeper source of creativity that allowed their minds the freedom to explore, and their hands to produce artistic original works. Harold John Coombs seemed destined for a more adventurous life right from the outset of his birth on November 13, 1883.[12] His father was a civil engineer in England, who built bridges among other constructions. This, of course, required uprooting the family with the completion of each project. However, the constant moving enabled Coombs to gain considerable knowledge of a wide cross section of life.

First homestead built by Coombs

With the call of freedom and opportunity fresh in his veins in the early 1900s, Coombs ventured to the prairies, first becoming employed as a hired hand with a rancher in the Broadview area. Soon, however, he staked his own homestead claim on the west side of Meeting Lake, proving it in 1925. He later moved directly west of the village of Maymont.[13] Like most settlers in the area, this meant he had to travel to North Battleford for supplies.

Second set of buildings

Straightaway Coombs constructed a log house, which he referred to as his "shack," and then a log stable for the four white horses that he soon acquired. He never owned much in the way of livestock otherwise, depending almost entirely on his beloved four-legged animals

Hand-carved ducks—wall decoration

until 1956, being one of the last in the district to resort to tractor power.[14]

During the winter months, and whenever he wasn't farming, he occupied his time with woodworking, securing materials from the trees and roots on his farm. Once he relinquished his horses, Coombs spent more time than ever carving knick-knacks from roots, figures of all kinds from bits of wood as well as animals, birds, and whatever else might strike his fancy.[15]

Although other people in the area might travel south to obtain different kinds of woods, Coombs resorted to securing what he needed from his own habitat. He delighted visitors by hanging carved monkeys in trees, and displaying alligators and snakes in the grass throughout his farmyard.

At one point he attempted some diamond willow work. A stand of his still exists. He also made a music stand, a mermaid shelf, a ballerina/skater, and a penguin.[16] At one point he carved a pair of ducks, made for hanging on the wall.[17]

Coombs seemed to have a discerning eye for creating both the "absurd" and the lifelike. When he espied a particular piece of wood or a dislodged root, he knew immediately what it was to become. He

Monkeys that hung from the trees in his yard (WDM-73-NB-2467, WDM-73-NB-2468)

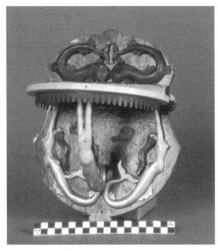

Mermaid Shelf (WDM-73-NB-2465)

had the ability to harness this particular brand of creativity, using the crudest of tools to fashion his artifacts.

His main objective seems to have been personal amusement. He never intended his items for sale, but he did give them away.

★ ★ ★

Both Coombs and Smith, it seems, carried a similar strain of thought or creativity, giving of themselves, yet in diverse ways, and for different purposes. Certainly, Coombs was able to manufacture furnishings for his personal needs as well as following his own inner urgings to create fanciful artifacts. Smith on the other hand, used his abilities to create simple, yet sturdy serviceable furnishings from next to nothing in the way of building materials, enhancing them to the best of his capabilities while faced with sometimes severe limitations.

These men despite the conditions, survived using their wits and some found inner strength to persevere. Today their work remains a prime example of the embodiment of the true pioneer spirit. Through their artifacts, and that of others like them, future generations will marvel at the magnitude of the ingenuity and fortitude of creativity, at work well done.

Alligator, skater, diamond willow stand, penguin and music stand (Western Development Museum artifacts)

1. Vocation and date of birth from his birth certificate.

2. The local history book says he came in 1914, however on further speaking with Campbell Smith, he recalls mention of his father being in Regina at the time of the cyclone in 1912.

3. Land description: N ½ of 14-13-4-W3.

4. From *Harvest of Memories: R. M. 134 and Shamrock,* (Shamrock: Shamrock History Society, 1990), p. 52.

5. The last of the W Bar Ranching Company Limited was let for settlement in 1925, according to the Shamrock History Book, p. 53.

6. Alice had been working at the University of Saskatoon since coming to Canada with her family in 1913, according to the Shamrock History Book, *Harvest of Memories,* p. 727.

   (B.E.S.L. stands for British Ex-Service League)

7. They had several hired women at different times.

8. Quote from his son, Campbell Smith.

9. *Harvest of Memories, R.M. 134 and Shamrock,* p. 727.

10. This piece belongs to his son, Campbell Smith at Coderre.

11. Alice passed away on May 10, 1986 at the age of 93.

12. The year of his birth date is found in the Maymont history book, but his tombstone says 1885. Franklin Mohler, one of Coombs' friends says he may actually have been born in Wales, because he was quite familiar with the area, especially Conway Castle.

13. His first homestead was on the NW 32-48-12-W3rd, according to his neighbour and friend Franklin Mohler. He later moved to the NE of 31.

14. The log stable was donated to the Western Development Museum at North Battleford.

15. Several of these artifacts are held in the Western Development Museum in Saskatoon.

16. Many of these artifacts are housed in the Western Development Museum in Saskatoon.

17. These are in a private collection.

Individual
WOODWORK

ABRAHAMSON, ERIC (1877–1976)

Erick Abrahamson was born on August 15, 1877, in Offerdal, Jampland, Sweden. He immigrated to Canada in 1903 to the Percival area. He later took out a homestead near Kipling on 22-14-5-W2. He was a carpenter by trade, building homes, barns, hotels, and schools. He also made furniture.

Abrahamson bookcase

ADDISON, JAMES (?–1963)

Originally from Liverpool, England, James Addison immigrated to Saskatoon in 1907 with his wife

Addison sod house

Jane and two children. He was a skilled carpenter, and from 1907 to 1909 he worked in Saskatoon building a collegiate and a brewery. From there he moved to the Kindersley area at Beadle in 1910, where he built a sod house, and other children were born.

They lived in a lean-to until the sod house was completed in 1911. He then made all the furnishings for inside his home. The home is still standing and occupied, and has been declared a heritage site.

ANDERSON, ELOF JOHN (1904–1979)

Elof John Anderson was a skilled carpenter from Dubuc, who made all his own furniture, including cupboards, chairs, tables and benches, as well as skids, toboggans, rocking horses, and toy boxes.

He made most of his furniture from trees hewn in the Qu'Appelle Valley. He was known

Anderson table made from an apple cart
(See back cover for underside)

to be able to make "something from nothing" like the knick-knack table above, made from an apple box.

ARMBRUSTER, JACOB A. (1854-1935)

Of German ancestry, Jacob Armbruster was born at Gassendorf, Austria (now in Poland), in 1854 to Johan Armbruster and Katharina Lutz. In 1893 he immigrated to a small farm near Neudorf, then he and his wife, Anna (1855-1941), and their son moved into town in 1905.

He began work as a carpenter's apprentice about 1868 in Drohob-

Armbruster tools

ystch, Austria, for four years until he became a journeyman. He produced all types of cupboards, tables and cabinets throughout his life in the Neudorf area. He made his own tools, including a set of planes, which he brought with him to Canada. He died on January 5, 1935, of anemia.

ARMSTRONG, BARTLEY MERRET (1870-1939)

The Armstrong's had lived in New York and Pennsylvania for several generations before moving to Minnesota. There on March 4, 1870, Bartley Merret Armstrong was born and later moved to

Buffalo, North Dakota, where the family homesteaded between 1914 and 1925. He later moved with his family to Meadow Lake on October 31, 1928, where they resided on their home quarter (SE 9-60-18-W3).

Armstrong ironing board and chair

ASHLEY, ARTHUR (?-1961)

Arthur Ashley was a cabinetmaker in England. He immigrated in 1912, homesteading on NE 26-14-24-W3 in the Kindersley area. He made all of his own furniture. He also built coffins, including his own. He received $15.00 to $35.00 for them from the town office

Ashley chairs

until his services were no longer needed. After he retired in the late thirties, he moved to Calgary where he continued to make, repair furniture and build kitchen cupboards. He also made whimsical furniture such as chairs from animal horns.

BAKER, NILES A. (?-?)

Of Irish descent, Niles Baker came to the Tiny area before WWI via North Dakota. A "fine work" carpenter, he built a tabernacle for the newly built church (Transfiguration of Our Lord Jesus Christ) Ukrainian Catholic Church north of Tiny in 1933. He also did fine work in cafés whenever they were remodelled.

BENOIT, CHARLES ALBERT (1882-?)

Charles Benoit was born in Ottawa on April 7, 1882. On November 22, 1906, he married Anna Vaillant, born in 1886, and they had at least two sons and one daughter, Jeanne, born in 1922 in Saskatchewan. She later became Jeanne Sauve, Speaker of the House of Commons.

He immigrated to the Howell district in Saskatchewan in 1919. This is now the town of Prud'homme. While there he built barns in the area and in Prud'homme he worked on the convent, and built the steeple and the pillars on either side of the Saints Donatien and Rogatien Parish Church in 1922. He found making a living in Saskatchewan too difficult and returned to Ottawa with his family in 1925.

BERG, FRANK (?-?)

Frank Berg came from Russia to Canada in 1903 via the U.S. He built his farmhouse in 1904 and became a Canadian citizen in 1906. He built the elevator in Langham, helped install the hardwood floors at the Normal School (Teacher's College) in Saskatoon and made quite a number of furniture pieces, including those with inlay work. He learned his trade in Russia and his work is available only in private collections.

CALDWELL DAVID (CA. 1871-?)

David Caldwell came to the Neet area in 1931. He moved to Meadow Lake were he continued to make his willow furniture. He would cut the willows, peel them

Benoit church

Caldwell bench owned by the Yake family

and place them on a homemade rack to dry. He used only a jack-knife, a saw and a hammer. He used very little nails, and sometimes he fastened his pieces with silver-coloured wire. He made rocking chairs, stools, small tables, and a loveseat for the Yake family.

CHARLES, RICHARD LUDLOW (?-?)

Richard Ludlow was born in Aberdeen, Scotland, where he was trained in woodworking. He later immigrated to Canada, where he was the CPR freight agent in Moosomin for many years.

He married and had one son and a daughter, and was an excellent band master. In the late 1920s he organzied the first band in Moosomin, and encouraged girls to join. This was also a first. During his lifetime he made cabinets and violins, and in 1926 he made the pulpit and communion table for St. Andrews' Presbyterian Church in Moosomin. He died in Regina.

CUNNINGHAM, DAVID A. (?-?)

David Cunningham came from Huntington, Quebec to join his brother at Broadview in 1877. Cunningham homesteaded his own land east of Kipling at NE 22-13-5 W2. He was a carpenter by trade who built homes and farms for the settlers from 1897 to 1905, after which time he moved to B.C. He also made cabinets, tables and other furnishings, besides game tables like this pool table in Kipling.

Charles church interiors

Cunningham pool table

DANCHILLA, JOHN (CA. 1903-1979)

John Danchilla was born on a homestead near Canora in 1903 or 1904, to George and Garagina Danchilla, who had previously immigrated from Romania. His birth was registered at Tetlock Post Office, North-West Territory—now Canora. He was raised in the Canora area and married Eileen Gullason in 1935. They had three sons.

He worked for an oil company and then was employed with Saskatchewan Co-op Creamery Association between 1949-1968. He also farmed and enjoyed playing the violin, besides doing his woodwork, which was mostly a hobby that included fretwork and some carving.

Danchilla furniture

He was self-taught and used coping or fret saws, chisels, files, and a lathe to fashion pieces out of wood scraps, orange and apple crates, and cheap lumber. Mostly he worked on the fretwork inside the house during the long winter months, but made furniture outside in his shop in the warmer times. He made furniture such as a rocker, chair, a footstool, and a table, as well as fretwork shelves, pipes, crosses, and curios.

Danchilla cornershelf

DE BASTIEN, ROCAN (?-?)

Rocan De Bastian came to the Rocanville area in the early 1880s. He originally farmed, but was foresighted in moving and establishing a village, which was named after him in 1903/04. He became the first overseer. He built functional woodwork as needs demanded. A chair that he built is on display in the Rocanville Museum.

De Bastien chair

DORSCH, JOSEPH (?-?)

Little is known about Joseph Dorsch, except that he lived at Ituna, was married and had some family. One of the few known pieces in existence of his work today is a corner wall cupboard, which is in a private collection.

Dorsch corner cupboard

DUPRAU, JAMES ARTHUR (1860-1947)

James Duprau was born July 5, 1860, at Riverside (Morrisburg), Ontario. His father was a French Roman Catholic and his mother a young Irish Orangewoman. He married Alberta Henrietta Green, and they had seven sons and one daughter.

He worked on the railroad in his early years, travelling in Iowa, Minnesota, North and South Dakota, returning to Canada in 1884. He learned his carpentry trade from his (then future) father-in-law, John Green, in Toronto, Ontario. In 1896 he moved his family to Regina, and then to Grenfell.

He took an active interst in politics, being an ardent Tory. He also managed the rink, and was fire inspector and building inspector for some years. Both he and his wife were active members in the Anglican Church.

He earned his living as a builder and a carpenter, but may have also made furniture. In Grenfell he built the Masonic Temple, his house on Anderson Street, the first town rink in 1896, the Kings' Hotel before it was destroyed by fire in 1927, plus many of the houses in town and the surrounding area. In the latter years he operated a paint and repair shop.

ERIKSON, JONAS
(?-?)

Jonas Erikson was a native of Sweden, who immigrated to Canada in 1903, settling in the Pierceland district of north-central Saskatchewan. He was married with a family. He created carvings, which tell the simple story of the settlement of the West, such as buildings, vehicles and animals, which are replicas of his own farmstead days up until the year 1913.

Erikson miniatures

FESSER, JOHN
(?-?)

A German by birth, John Fesser came from Neudord, Austria, immigrating with his family to the Neudorf/Killaly area in approximately 1891. He was married and had a wife and eight children. He made china cabinets, wardrobes, tables and other household furniture. The Fessers eventually moved to MacKinson's Landing, B.C., in the 1930s when they were quite old.

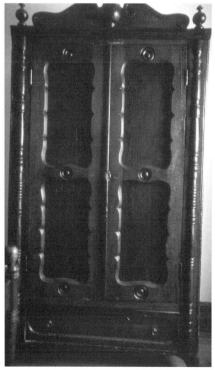

Fesser wardrobe

GAUTHIER, FERDINAND (?-1948)

Born at Weedon, Quebec, Ferdinand Gauthier moved to Cantal, Saskatchewan, four miles north and half a mile west of Gravelbourg in 1905. He made toys, children's furniture, picture frames and many kinds of sculpting after his retirement in 1916.

HAMMOND, GEORGE (1860-1949)

George Hammond originally came to Canada in 1887 from Aylseford, Kent, England. A carpenter by trade, he was asked to do the woodwork on Regina's first prison on the lakeshore. Next he was asked to go to Maple Creek to erect a building at the NWMP barracks, in the early 1890s. He built the long benches and desks for the log school at Hay Creek, where his children attended school. In 1903 he worked for the government building bridges, and he also helped with the first ferry at Mongomery's Landing one hundred miles north of Maple Creek. An original counter was hand-carved with a jackknife, and built by George Hammond and either John Harvey or Ted Perrin, depending on the sources sited, in 1883 in Maple Creek for the Dixon Brothers store.

HAZLEBOWER, ? (?-?)

Mr. ? Hazlebower worked in the Hafford/Krydor area of the province. He was married with several sons. He's known mostly for the work he did on the St. Michael's Church, including the many icons, candleholders, small church replicas to hold the euchirist, as well as other decorations.

Hammond and Perrin counter

St. Michael's Church interior

HODEL, JACOB
(1880-1918)

Jacob Hodel was born on February 12, 1880, in Itzkany, Austria. He homesteaded in the Lajord area, where he built a sod house. He married Elizabeth Tiefenbach on August 20, 1903. (She was born in Poland.)

Hodel frames

They had three girls and two boys. He enjoyed singing in the church choir, and playing the button accordion. He sewed his own suits, and knit socks and mitts by the light of a coal oil lamp. He seemed to have some knowledge of farming, but did woodworking on the side. He was particularly proficient with a jackknife as well. Mostly he worked with wood as a hobby, using wooden cigar boxes for material. He died at the Grey Nuns Hospital in Regina on December 10, 1918, at the age of 38 from a ruptured appendix.

HOWARD, JOHN
(1877-1966)

John Howard was born December 4, 1877, to Thomas and Alice Howard at Shankey Hall, Warrington, Lancaster, England. In early May of 1884 he immigrated with his parents to the Whitewood area, in the St. Luke School District. He married Sophie McKenzie on May 24, 1906 at St. Matthew's Anglican Church. They lived on SE 27-17-2-W2, where they had five children.

In about 1911, he made a camera in which he used glass negatives. He also made his own developing outfit and became the photographer for the area. He enjoyed playing the violin (so did his wife), read *National Geographic,* and dabbled in astronomy.

Besides being a qualified steam engineer, John was a blacksmith, who at one time sharpened ploughshares for 25 cents. In the early 1900s the Howards needed furniture, so he made a lathe to turn the legs and rungs. He had a small sawmill for producing his own lumber. He used birch and burr oak from the Qu'Appelle Valley.

He made thirty violins, two cellos and a double bass violin, a bishop's chair, prayer stool and other furniture such as tables with inlay. He died of a heart attack on June 20, 1966.

Howard chair

Howard instrument

Jasieniuk, Joseph (1890–1935)

Joseph Jasieniuk was born in Lubow, Austria. In his late teens he went job-hunting in Brazil, but immigrated to Canada a year later, settling in the Krydor area. To supplement his income he built a buckwheat mill, millet mill, flour mill, grain cleaner, saw mill, lathe, and a diecast for making concrete monuments. His wood works are still visible in the form of church alters, benches, candle holders and other artifacts in the area.

Kadyba, John (?–ca. 1880s)

John Kadyba, probably of Polish ancestry, came to Canada in 1924 as a young man. It was thought that he was married and had a family. He was very poor, but eventually had a farm in the Krydor/Blaine Lake area. One winter he lived two miles straight north of the church, which was eleven miles south and half a mile west of Krydor.

During the summer months, he built churches in the area. In the winter he had agreements with people to build furniture, kitchen cupboards, benches, sideboards,

Kadyba bureau

wardrobes, etc. in trade for board and room. He decorated his work using a set of floral punches he owned. A wheat sheaf is one of his known designs. He is buried in the Bear Lake Church cemetery.

Kashtalanych, Alec (?–1937)

The only piece of furniture that is known of Alex Kashtalanych is a bench built in 1935. It is surmised that he was married with at least one son, and came from the Wroxton area. He died in 1937 before his son was born.

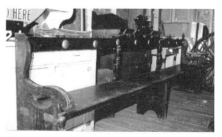
Kashtalanych bench

KLEISINGER, JOSEPH
(1874-1960)

Joseph Kleisinger's name in his homeland of Hungary was spelled Geisinger, but by error the G was changed to K and never corrected upon immigrating to Regina in 1903. In 1912 he built the first dance hall in Regina at 1745 Ottawa St. He organized a family orchestra and wrote his own songs. He was a carpenter by trade, who made his own furniture. He also built barns, houses, etc., working from 1903 until his retirement.

KRIPKI, SAMUEL
(1883-1970)

Samuel Kripki was born in Ukraine in 1883. In about 1920 he moved to the Colonsay/Elstow area after spending some time in Newark, New Jersey. His wife was Justina Baetoshiw (1877-1966), whom he wed in 1911. They had six children.

Kripki cupboard

He taught children to write and read Ukrainian during the winter months, moving from farmhouse to farmhouse, where there were approximately eleven to fifteen students at each place. He planted orchards and enjoyed tree grafting as hobby. He also loved horses and was a good farmer. When he retired from the farm, he moved into Saskatoon where he raised chickens until he was caught and forced to quit. He also built little sheds in the back of people's yards.

He used scraps and whatever materials were at hand to make breadbox cupboards, stools, tables, trunks, and other things of necessity. He died in 1970.

KROCHAK, WASYL (WILLIAM) (1891-1971)

Krochak stand

William Krochak was born at Sapohiw, Ternopole, Ukraine, on March 9, 1891. He immigrated to Vita, Manitoba, and then took a homestead at Arran, Saskatchewan, on Section 15-36-30. He married and had three boys and five girls.

He liked doing cross-stitch needlework and embroidered the local priest's cloak, made rugs and sewed dresses for his daughters. He enjoyed working with wood, but was not keen on farming. A thoughtful, kind-hearted man, he and his sons each played a different musical instrument for their own entertainment.

Krochak paintings

Krochak church interior

He helped build the Ukrainian Catholic church at Whitebeech, including many of the pieces inside, such as the pews, altar, etc. He also did decorative painting in his own house. He used spruce and birch, which he cured himself. He made furniture for other people, but seldom for payment, because of the enjoyment it gave him to work with wood.

LAWRENCE, WILLIAM F.
(?-?)

In the 1880s and 1890s William Lawrence had a sash and door company, and also made caskets when an accident or untimely death occurred, but he didn't build furniture. He was a skilled carpenter, who later opened a furniture store, and was the first "undertaker" in the area. He died in the 1950s at the age of 93.

LEVORSON, KNUT
(?-1958)

Knut Levorson arrived in the Battram area by train in 1917 from Dunseith, North Dakota. He originally came from Tunnhovd, a small community in Numedal, Norway, in 1901. He worked from 1909 to

Levorson violin

1937 making violins. He also built a grain grinder in Saskatoon, and a postcard maker, which is located in the Yorkton Museum. He built fourteen violins, making everything except the strings. He even carved the posts.

LOON LAKE TOY CO-OPERATIVE
(CA. 1939-1941)

In the early 1930s approximately one hundred and fifty families settled in the St. Walburg/Loon Lake/Bright Sand/Goodsoil area. They were a community of Sudaten Germans who came from the Hungarian-Austrian Empire.

They established small communities where several families lived on one farm, such as the Tomlinson farm at Loon Lake.

Franz Rewald, Heinrich Palme, Anton Hocher, and Emil Hecht

Seven families, all with small numbers of children, lived in the Loon Lake community. Many had had responsible, industrialized jobs in the country they'd come from, such as mechanics and factory workers. When they came to Canada they had a difficult time becoming farmers, dealing with livestock and living in the bush on the poor farmland they acquired. They often turned to other means for supplementing their incomes.

Five men established the Loon Lake Toy Factory: Johan Merz (not shown in the photo above), Franz Rewald, Heinrich Palme, Anton Hocher, and Emil Hecht. Others may also have helped them in their enterprise. Of them all, Johan Merz was the only one with any experience working in a toy factory in his home country. Although the toy factory only existed for a couple of years, their pieces were well-crafted and the items popular. They made toys such as pull-toys in the shapes of chickens, chicks, ducks, and rabbits, also rocking horses, small boxes, whirligigs, and garden ornaments.

F. Lehnert and Franz Rewald with a Selection of Toys

Loon Lake Toy Factory Workshop

NISBET, REVEREND JAMES (1823–1874)

The son of a shipbuilder, Rev. James Nisbet was born in Glasgow. He trained as a carpenter under the tutelage of his father, continuing in Glasgow until 1844 when the family immigrated to Canada. He later became ordained as a Presbyterian Minister and in 1866 he accepted a call to found a mission in the North-West Territory of Canada. Some consider him the founder of Prince Albert. However, there is some discrepancy in sources that state that his cousin James Isbister was the founder, having arrived four years before James did. Nisbet helped build schools and churches in the area, and did other wood-work, including furniture.

Nisbet table

NOSTBAKKEN SR., GJERT NELSON (1867–1949)

Gjert Nostbakken Sr. was born in Norway on April 18, 1867. He immigrated to Story City, Iowa, in 1896, then moved to Carpio, North Dakota, in 1906 and finally in 1915, he took out a homestead in the Aneroid/Makota area on the SE ¼-16-6-10-W3. He and his wife, Anna, had several children.

He loved the look of wood and never used power tools. He was a lay preacher in the Norwegian language, and the family lived in a fairly isolated area of the province. He never owned a car, preferring to travel all his life with horses. He was a finishing carpenter on board ships before leaving Norway and may have had some formal training.

He built small furniture for people, houses and barns, church

As a business venture they were unsuccessful because they had no marketing skills and they were too far from a major centre. They used local lumber, usually birch that the workers seasoned themselves. This in itself, because the wood took so long to season before they could begin work, resulted in them closing down.

Loon Lake rocking horse

McDONALD, MALCOLM (1868–1952)

Originally the McDonalds came from the Isle of Lewis in Scotland, but had been living in Ontario,

McDonald couch and chair

around Stokes Bay, for a couple of generations. Malcolm was born in Canada in 1868. He came to Saskatchewan in 1905, settling eleven miles north of Southey.

He married Elizabeth Catherine McLeigh McLoy on March 1. 1899. They had several children. He died of cancer on June 9, 1952, while on a visit to his daughter in Gulf Bay, Ontario. His body was shipped back to Saskatchewan for burial.

McDonald carved heads

In 1909 he built his stonehouse and then made all the furniture in it. Many of the pieces were carved. He had no formal training in art, stone masonry or woodwork. He was a farmer who did woodworking on the side, often using poplar, willow and orange and apple crates.

He used a jackknife to carve dolls or doll heads made of firewood from the wood box. He hand-carved chairs, picture frames, a couch and armchair, as well as other furniture. He also painted pictures to decorate the family home.

McJANNET, JOHN
(CA.1862–1911)

John McJannet was born about 1862 to John and Mary Nelson McJannet. His biographical information is rather sketchy, but it's believed he had a wife, Hannah Jane, and may have had a daughter named Celia, who died in 1914.

Although his training or education his unknown, it appears he knew his craft. He, along with George Parley, built the St. Andrew's Anglican Church at Ceylon in 1889, and together they also built some of the first grain elevators in Grenfell. McJannet

McJannet cupboard

constructed many buildings and homes in and around Grenfell with various partners.

He earned his living as a carpenter and may have done other pieces, including furniture, on the side. He used the woods available from the local lumberyard, and in his own house made built-in cupboards. He died on July 13, 1911 in a construction accident, building the Walters Store on Desmond Street in Grenfell. He was 49. His wife then married William Cooper, a Grenfell chef.

NELSON, ERNEST
(1876–1940)

Ernest Nelson in his home, built entirely by hand.

Ernest Nelson was born in England in 1876. He came to Canada prior to 1890, via Argentina where he worked as a gaucho for a while. He joined his brother, Tom, near Baring (Glenavon district) and took out a homestead on the NW ¼-14-15-9-W2. His brother Tom eventually moved in with him. They had a sister who remained in England.

A nervous man, Ernest was wary of other people and rarely did woodwork outside his home. A few known exceptions are the porch on the Wolf Creek School in the

Tom & Ernest Nelson in their first home

Glenavon district, and lat on a veranda on a hous Moffat area (south of Wols and his brother read extens donated eight hundred l start the Glenavon library.

He was a master "shij so probably had some training. He had tools tha to put the oakem betw planking of wooden ships had wooden block plan chest with draw knives a tools. His home was si every corner used, includi in shelves, drawers and cuj

Nelson clamp

Ernest Nelson suffer severe migraine headaches he and his brother went to Island, B.C., for a time, but to Saskatchewan where the new house. They never m because Ernest died first. I mitted suicide with a shotg old home in 1940.

Nostbakken Sr. tools

Nostbakken Sr. dresser

pews, and coffins. He had a shop on his farm for woodworking. He used utilitarian, inexpensive woods—in many cases not necessarily good wood—and it may have needed paint. Most lumber was bought from the local lumberyard. He did more carpentry than farming, making such furniture as chests, wardrobes, washstands, and cupboards. He made his own wood lathe, spindles, tools such as wood planes, coffins for the municipality, pews for the Holiness Movement Church, and other items in Pointex. He died October 14, 1949, of a stroke at his home.

NOSTBAKKEN JR., GJERT NELSON (1894–1975)

Gjert Nostbakken Jr. was born in Moster, Norway to Anna and Gjert Nelson Nostbakken on October

19, 1894. He immigrated with his parents to the U.S., finally settling in Saskatchewan in the Aneroid district, homesteading on SE ¼-9-7-10-W3.

In 1926 he was married to Veda, a lady from North Dakota. He was an all around craftsman, who did everything from cement work, chimney building and farming to interior finishing, as well as blacksmithing. He also loved to visit and talk with people.

worked in people's homes and had his own workshop.

He built small pieces of furniture, built-in cupboards, did lathe work, built his own tools, chests, a Morris chair, a washstand, and did interior renovations of homes and businesses. He also made items for use around his own home, such as a swing for his children and skis for the family. He died of cancer on July 16, 1975, in the Kincaid Hospital.

Nostbakken Jr. in workshop

He was a self-taught carpenter and cabinetmaker, no doubt learning some tips from his father. He worked on the airport in Mossbank, building hangars, etc. for a while in the 1930s. He also

Nostbakken Jr. washstand

NOVECOSKY, JACOB
(1862-1928)

Of Hungarian descent, Jacob Novecosky was born in 1862 near Mariupol, Russia, by the Black Sea. His father's name was Martin. In 1904, he immigrated to Canada with his parents, his wife and family. They homesteaded seven miles south of Humboldt (one mile south of Bay Trail, once a hamlet.) His wife was Helen, who died in 1950

Second home, later his workshop

at the age of 82. They were married in the 1880s and had eleven children in Russia. The five oldest died in 1895 during a diphtheria epidemic, and another died on the ship coming over. Five more children were born in Canada.

On the train from Halifax to Winnipeg, all his savings were stolen, about $600, a lot of money in those days. All he had were his 70- and 63-year-old parents, his wife, the five remaining children, aged two to twenty, his carpentry tools, and a few clothes.

He built a sod house, barn and granary, then later a log-and-straw shelter for his carpentry. But a few years later lightning struck the building and all his tools went up in flames. In 1910 he built a second house with homemade mud bricks, then, in 1919, a third house of wood.

He was a carpenter by trade and a wheelwright, who travelled from place to place, when he wasn't farming. He used fir from the lumber yard, scraps of wood and apple boxes. He built barns and houses for settlers, also wagon wheels, buggies, picture frames, cupboards, tables, chairs, benches, and othe furniture.

He also made wooden crosses and built coffins, charging $5.00 for each. The first was for his father Martin in 1909 and the last for himself. In 1927 he became ill with cancer and he died in 1928 at the age of 66. He is buried in the St. Scholastic cemetery.

Novecosky's funeral—he built his own coffin.

PAQUIN, LORENZO (1882–1932)

Lorenzo Jean-Baptiste Paquin was born at Deschambault, Quebec, on March 17, 1882. Lorenzo had a wife and ten children.

While living in Iroquois Falls, Ontario, he worked at Abitibi Power and Pulp. After a huge fire went through Iroquois Falls in 1918, Paquin immigrated to Saskatchewan. First he went to Blucher on Section 13-36-W3. He then lived in Prud'homme for a time, and then in Saskatoon. He was a carpenter by trade, probably learning from other woodworkers. While in Saskatoon he worked at St. Paul's Hospital as a cabinetmaker and furniture repairman in 1923 and 1924. He also did furniture making for others in the Blucher and Prud'homme areas, and may have worked on various buildings.

Woodworking and carpentry was how he made his living. Besides construction, he also made cupboards, chairs, a rocking chair, other furniture, and several violins. He also played the violin.

Paquin rocking chair

He found it too difficult to make a living in Saskatchewan and returned to the east, leaving one daughter behind with her new husband. He died in February, 1932, in Windsor, Ontario, of cancer at the age of 50.

PARLEY, GEORGE ELLIOTT (1870-1949)

George Parley was born on September 10, 1870, at Scroghill, Old Deer, Aberdeenshire, Scotland, the first child of George Parley, a farm servant, and Mary Ann Simpson.

In 1890 at the age of 20, he came to Saskatchewan with an uncle, homesteading in what was known as the Baring district on SE 14-15-9, proving it in 1892. When his parents, brothers and sisters joined him in 1896, he surrendered the homestead to his father and took up residence in Grenfell where he was in demand as a carpenter. He had worked as a carpenter's apprentice until he qualified as a Master Carpenter in Scotland.

Annie Davidson of Rora, Aberdeenshire, Scotland became his bride on October 25, 1906. They had four children, two of whom (a one- and a half-year-old son and an eighteen-day-old daughter) died on the same day in April of 1909 of diphtheria. The other two sons lived to adulthood.

He was on the town council from 1916 to 1920, then for a term beginning in 1923, and from 1926 to 1933. He also served as the Mayor of Grenfell for a term from 1934 to 1937.

In 1889 he completed work on St. Andrew's Anglican Church in Ceylon with another carpenter named McJannet. He also helped McJannet build the first grain elevators in Grenfell in 1905 and beyond. When John McJannet died in a construction accident in 1911, George's brother, Jack became his partner.

Parley workshop. The smaller building is the workshop, while the windmill was their source of power. The brick building was the Windsor Theatre Block, formerly the Masonic Hall

The Catholic Mission Boarding School north of Broadview may have been built by the Parleys. They also built many homes for new settlers, accomplishing them in one-day stints.

In 1913, the Parley brothers became agents for farm machines. That same year, a power plant was started in Grenfell and George operated it for the first sixteen months. He and his brother Jack also opened a garage on Front Street in Grenfell. "The Parley Block," a building in Grenfell, is named after George and his brother.

The Parleys made fancy cabinets with mortise doors and panels in them for the armoury in Grenfell, but not long after they were installed the armoury burnt to the ground. George designed all the pieces he built, and always made sure his saws were sharp. One year he built a desk for the dentist in town, and another time he built a circular staircase for a grand home outside of Grenfell. George measured it up, built it in their shop, and then installed it for a perfect fit to the amazement of the owners.

George was fond of fishing and hunting. He built the first and only steamboat on Crooked Lake, which he called the "Pretoria."

Parley boat "Pretoria"

With Grenfell being easily accessible along a major rail line, the Parleys had access to a lumber yard and obtained most of their supplies there, carrying their boards across their shoulders through town to their workshop. George died November 8, 1949, in Grenfell and was predeceased by his wife in 1927.

PARLEY, JOHN (JACK/JOCK) (1878-1948)

John Parley was born on December 5, 1878, at Scroghill, Old Deer, Aberdeenshire, Scotland, the fifth child of George Parley, a farm servant, and Mary Ann Simpson. He immigrated to Saskatchewan with his parents and siblings in 1896 at the age of 17. The next summer he was old enough to take out a homestead, which he did on SE 10-15-9-W2 near Glenavon. He gained entry in 1898 and received the patent in 1902.

He remained single, and was an ambitious man. He acquired a threshing outfit and was able to supplement his income threshing for his neighbours. With a passion for hunting pheasant, he kept his family well supplied with wild fowl. He always kept hunting dogs and loved curling, often wearing an outsized Scots tam o'shanter. He had a collection of butterflies mounted in a cabinet of glass-covered drawers. He also had mounted birds in glass cabinets. He was kind-hearted and entertaining, enjoying a drink or two, which earned him the reputation as the "black sheep" of the family.

He apprenticed with his brother George, often working in the summer during the first years after immigrating to Saskatchewan. He joined him full-time in 1912 in Grenfell, choosing to give up his homestead. He often did the planing and sanding for George, but also had a reputation as a fine carpenter.

Note the intricate cupboard above Jack Parley's head.

In July of 1914 he purchased a Studebaker motorcar and eventually the Parley brothers (he and his brother George) opened a garage, which Jack took over. He also began

A table built by the Parleys

dealing in cars. He died on February 13, 1948, in Grenfell from complications after breaking a leg. (For more information on the Parley work, please refer to George Parley.)

PEASE, GEORGE
(?-?)

George Pease was a pioneer boatman at Lake Waskesiu, Prince Albert National Park. He made hand-made chairs from naturally crooked trees about 1926/27 like the one below. A similar one was made for Joseph Wood, the first superintendent of the Park.

Pease chair

PERRIN, EDWIN (TED)
(1870-1961)

Born at Aylseford, Kent, England, Ted Perrins family originally came to Canada in 1887 with others, including his cousin George Hammond's family. He later partnered with George on his homestead on NW ¼-9-28-25. (See Hammond, George for photo of Dixon Brothers store counter, which he co-built)

ROGERS, SAMUEL (1872-1961)

The Rogers family originally came from England, but several generations had lived in the U.S. or eastern Canada. Samuel was born on January 2, 1872, in Hollen, Ontario. His father George was a carpenter, as was his grandfather Augustus, and great-grandfather Timothy Rogers. Timothy came from the U.S. in the early 1800s. Before leaving, he'd built the Quaker Church in New Market, which is still used today.

Samuel left Ontario for Fleming, spent a short time in B.C. working in a furniture shop, then returned to Saskatchewan because the damp weather in B.C. irritated his asthma. For a brief time he also

Library desk

went back to Ontario, finally settling in Saskatchewan for good.

He began carpentry work at Fleming. Between 1911 and 1915 he worked for his uncle Stewart Bartleman in Regina. They built the Bartleman Apartments. He then moved to the Moose Mountain area where he set up his own sawmill at Kenosee Lake, using a George White steam engine to run the operation. He used birch and poplar lumber, most of which he sawed himself.

Rogers dresser

He made cupboards and furniture such as desks, tables, dressers, washstands, and bookcases. He also built houses, barns and trailers, and did finishing work in houses. He made his furniture with a "French" finish, applying coat after coat of hot linseed oil with a great deal of rubbing. Older pieces have nails with square heads. He was a full-time carpenter and cabinetmaker.

He married in 1900 and had several children. He died of pneumonia on November 11, 1961.

ROMAN, MARIE
(?-CA. 1973)

Marie Roman came from Romania to Wood Mountain, eventually living at Dysart. He had a wife and several children. He died in approximately 1973.

This Roman coffin is in storage in the Western Development Museum in Saskatoon [WDM-83-5-54 (55)]

It's known that Marie had a partner, a Mr. Bergan in Regina. It's also known that Johan Adolf, who started a lumber business in Dysart about 1923, first employed him. The area needed a coffin maker and apparently Mr. Adolf asked him to do it. Besides coffins, he probably did other woodworking.

RUSSELL, ARNOLD
(?-?)

Nothing much is known about Arnold Russell, except that he was from the Prince Albert area, and that he made pieces of furniture from recycled ship lumber. He also built an oak table constructed from wood given to him by various pioneer residents who have their names on the table on a brass plaque.

Russell table

SALO, JOHN HENRY
(1903-1970)
(No relation to Oscar Salo)

John Henry Salo (changed from Saloranta) was born at Isokyro, Finland, on January 12, 1903. In 1928 he immigrated to Dunblane, then moved to various places, including in the New Finland area, Rocanville, and then to B.C. in the later years.

Little is known about his early life, but he was probably a carpenter before he immigrated. He married Bertha Nieminen on May 21, 1945, in New Finland (between Whitewood and Tantallon), and they had one son.

In Dunblane he worked as a farmhand, trucker and in steam equipment operation. He then owned and operated a show repairshop at Macrorie. In 1933 he moved his business to Tantallon before opening one in Rocanville. He once tried to run a car by burning wood. He also did carpentry work, concentrating mostly on this type of employment from the 1940s until his death in Vancouver in 1970.

SALO, OSCAR
(1873-1966)

Oscar Salo was born in Finland, possibly in the town of Viipuri, in 1873. He came to Canada in 1915, settling in the New Finland area, a Finnish colony started about 1897 on the south side of the Qu'Appelle Valley between Whitewood and Tantallon.

It is believed that he was married in Finland and that he had one son. He never sent for his family, and if something happened to them before he immigrated, he never talked about it.

He worked for a time in B.C. on the CPR and rode the freight train. Finally he settled on the Salonen farmstead in the New

Finland area, as he had grown up with these people. He first built a log house, and later other buildings.

Oscar's home

He loved children and taught Salonen's daughter to play cribbage. Salo always carried peppermints in his pocket, and although he smoked in the early years, he later quit and chewed snuff instead.

Oscar Salo had a passion for making false bottoms in cupboards and had many hiding spots for his money, changing the places of concealment frequently. A bit of a loner, who drank occasionally, he never owned a vehicle or any land, but was well liked and friendly.

He was a talented carpenter, familiar with all aspects, but whether he had any formal training is not known. He had worked with birchbark since he was a boy. This was his favourite pastime. The birchbark containers he made had interlocking joins and many were typical Scandinavian designs.

Salo table

He built several houses out of log, then later of lumber, many of which still stand today. He also built the parsonage for the St. John's Lutheran Church with volunteer labour. He was responsible for cutting the church in half, by hand, when it was moved in 1934. He rejoined it with the join being barely visible.

Salo containers

Salo mostly used birch, birch-bark and ash, all found locally, which he cured. He made furniture of all types, birchbark containers for coffee, salt matches, tobacco and snuff, as well as trinket boxes, skis, wooden birch spoons and wall brackets. He crafted pieces with V-joints, and interlocking birchbark pieces without any nails in them.

He died in 1966 in Whitewood, having spent his last years with his friends, Charlie and Jenny Salonen. He is buried in the New Finland cemetery.

SAMUELS, FLORIAN TEODOR (RALPH) (1891-1960)

Samuels desk

Ralph Samuels was born Florea Teodor Samoil in Ostrita, Bukovina, Austria-Hungary. Of Romanian descent, his father was Eftodie Samoil with the name being anglicized to Teodor Samuels when they immigrated in 1899 to Canada. They sailed from the port of Hamburg to Halifax, venturing to the North-West Territory (Saskatchewan). They homesteaded on land which is now within the boundaries of the town of Canora (NE 24-30-4). Ralph was eight years old at the time.

On June 15, 1911, Ralph married Dominica Toedor Lodva at St. Maria Church in Canora. Although he did not have any formal education, he could speak six languages.

At the age of 15, Ralph Samuels

built a belfry on the local Romanian church (about 1905). Later he
built churches, homes, barns, and
furniture. He eventually established
the Samuels Construction Company.

Picture frame and box

Samuels dresser

He also built Eucharist churches
and other church icons. He produced anything out of wood that
customers wanted, even designs
found in a catalogue. He died on
May 6, 1960, of cancer in the
Canora Union Hospital.

STEVENS[ON] WILLIAM (?)
(?-?)

Although his name is not known
for certain, this fellow came from
England. His work reflects obvious
training, and today he would prob-

ably be classed as an industrial arts
teacher, or a professional chip
carver. He used stylized designs
(using a pattern board), and seemed
to make things for himself and his
family only. Pieces that survive
include a child's bureau, trinket
box, picture frames and cupboards.

SWENSON, NELS
(?-?)

Nels Swenson was born and raised in
Sweden. He never homesteaded, but
did work in the Broadview area during the 1930s. He had a wife and
children in Sweden. He and a
brother had been relying on the soup
kitchen in Regina, but went out to
the Broadview area to work on the
farms to earn their keep. He was
going to return to Sweden to con-

Swenson side table

he was probably a professional cabinetmaker. His work included buffets, china cabinets, tables, chairs, and bathroom cabinets.

vince his wife and family to move permanently to Canada with him.

His work reflects training, but his background is unknown, although

One winter, in the 1930s, he worked for a family in the Broadview area, building them a china cabinet and matching table. He was going to finish the chairs when he returned from his visit in Sweden, but met his untimely death, dying of pneumonia instead. He used birch from the nearby Pipestone valley.

Swenson wall cupboard

Swenson table and china cabinet

VANCE, ROBERT
(1844-1913)

Of Irish descent, Robert Vance was born on January 28, 1844 in Upper Canada. He left Lambton County, Ontario, in 1892 to homestead three miles north of Fleming on the NW ¼-22-13-30-W1. He married and had a family. One year, he attended the Brandon Fair about 1913 when cars were a novelty, he posed for his portrait.

He had knowledge of carpentry and stone masonry, used local poplar, and probably some wood from the lumber stores. He built a sod house and some of the furnishings for it in 1892 when he first homesteaded. Later he helped build the R.D. McNaughton store in Moosomin, and donated many hours of work to building the little stone Methodist Church at Fleming, now the United Church.

In 1893 he built a tailored fieldstone cottage for a Mr. Ives west of Elkhorn, Manitoba. He also became a steam engineer and was a partner in a steam threshing outfit for years. In 1899 he laid the fieldstone foundation walls of a large farm home for Davie McCormick and also did all the interior woodwork, which included all the banister spindles and newel posts.

The bottom post was of turned native oak, done to his own design on a hand-powered lathe. He died at Fleming on November 9, 1913.

Two chairs made by Vance out of poplar in 1892

Fleming Methodist Church

WENDEL, JACOB
(1883-1964)

Jacob Wendel was born on October 14, 1883 to Ludwig Jacob Wendel and Barbara Unterschutz from Styrj, Galicia, Austria. His family immigrated to Neudorf, Austria, about 1891, then to the Neudorf Colony near Hyde (a small community) in Saskatchewan when he was eight years old.

Jacob eventually owned a farm and then moved into town. His wife was Barbara Ulmer (1887-1957) and they had four daughters and two sons. Many of the streets in Neudorf are named after his children.

He had a shop in his yard on the east end of town. He made furniture, mostly for his own use, and caskets as needed. Some of these items included cupboards, china cabinets, sideboards, breadboxes, trunks, and fern stands. He also built barns and houses in the Neudorf, Killaly, Lemberg, and Grayson areas. He used cedar and other woods that he was able to find. He died in the Melville Hospital on October 26, 1964, and is buried in the Neudorf Cemetery.

This particular corner cupboard made by Wendel has been refinished from its original appearance

WILMOT, EDWARD (1880-1963)

Edward Wilmot was born at Slough, Buckinghamshire, England, on April 1, 1882. He immigrated to the Biggar/Maymont district and bought a farm from the CPR. His wife was Emily Harriet Flax (1878-1943). They had a son, William Henry (1904-1929), plus several daughters.

He was a bass singer in the local church choir, and played the organ. Although he was fairly poor, he never asked for help. His wife was a great support to him. He was versatile in building and woodworking, so probably had some training.

Wilmot lectern

He created and carved various pieces for the All Saints Anglican Church in Maymont, including the lectern in 1910, the pulpit and font in 1922, hymn board, book cabinet and chair stalls in 1929, communion table or altar in 1943, the missal in 1946, and the prayer desk in1947.

He also carved six text boards with the commandments. Later on, he carved the text boards for the Radisson, Fielding, and Maymont United Churches. He touched every bit of wood on the wall plaques, carving them in some way. Sometimes he was paid enough for materials, but the pieces in the

Wilmot collection

Wilmot pulpit

Maymont church were considered more a labour of love.

Sometimes he had special woods imported, but he usually used local materials. He was a woodcarver, furniture builder, cabinetmaker, carpenter, and bricklayer. He died of a heart attack in Kamloops, B.C., in August of 1963.

Wilmot plaque

WILSON, WILFRED JOHN (1882–1980)

John Wilson (as he was known locally) was the fourth child of Margaret Ann Walker and James William Wilson. He was born on January 5, 1882, at Swain Hill Terrace in Yeadon, near Leeds in Yorkshire, England. Both his parents came from Rawdon, Yorkshire.

At the age of ten, John went to work in a factory. Between 1900 and 1904, he obtained first-class certificates in the elementary subjects that make up professional drawing through the South Kensington Board of Education. He served his full apprenticeship in the craft of woodcarving at Keighley in England. He became a highly skilled woodcarver and draughtsman.

Wilson oval frame

When he left England, he moved to Toronto with his family. Then five years later, in 1910, he came to Saskatchewan, homesteading on the NE ¼-36-25-8-W2.

When he first immigrated to Toronto, he worked in a piano factory. Upon homesteading, he constructed a log cabin and carved everything inside that could possibly be carved.

John went back east to wed Eleanor (Nellie) Shipley Saulters on February 20, 1913, in Toronto. She was born on May 5, 1885, at Wokington, Cumberland, England. They returned to Saskatchewan where their union produced seven children.

John and Nellie were "doctor and nurse" to the locals, setting bones and delivering babies. Nellie knit and wove her own clothes from wool obtained from the sheep they raised. They lived in a ramshackle old log cabin, but never considered themselves poor. Instead, they made and distributed mitts and socks to needy neighbours, particularly for the Christmas of 1934.

They raised sheep, cattle, horses, pigs, chickens, and bees. John rode a bicycle and also could walk for miles. In the early years he was a harvester and did road work whenever possible to earn a little cash.

Wilson plaque with horns

Wilson boxes

He made the pulpit at the Wadena United Church, the mayor's chair in Saskatoon, and did some work at the Bessborough Hotel in Saskatoon. He also made the communion table, baptismal font and choir posts for the Grace United Church in Sturgis, and carved a mahogany wall plaque, which won a prize at the Pacific National Exhibition in Vancouver in 1952.

Wilson's prized pieces were the carved grandfather clocks that he

Wilson collection of frames

made for each members of his family, plus one for another couple. The inner workings for the clocks came from England, but he hand-carved the entire wooden parts, inside and out. They didn't have any nails in them.

He taught chip carving without pay at the local country school (Turnout), bicycling there on Friday afternoons. He made all one hundred of his wood chisels, including those for the children to use at the school. He designed his own patterns, but never used the same one twice, destroying them after he'd used them. On one occasion he demonstrated woodcarving for the Saskatchewan Arts Board Festival at Canora. In the early years he did work for the Regina Sash and Door Company, but for neighbours he did work at a nominal fee.

He carved everything that he did, usually with oak acorns, maple leaves, wild roses and ivy designs. He used light oak, mahogany, apple box ends, quarter-cut oak, and various other woods as they became available. He made various objects, such as church furnishings, wall plaques, paper racks, sewing stands, jewellery boxes, toy trains, coffins, pin cushions, mounted deer horns, violins, wooden spoons, picture frames, and matchbox holders. He also did carvings on pianos, lamps, figurines, and built a spinning wheel and his own lathe, which he ran with a bicycle apparatus.

His hobbies were watercolour painting and carving. He was a trustee and secretary-treasurer for the Turnout school district (near his home of Hazel Dell). Later he was president of the local Senior Citizens committee for two terms, a member of the Centennial Committee, and a member of the Volunteer Recreation Services in Rutland, B.C., where they retired in 1953.

He took up oil painting when he was almost blind, losing one eye to glaucoma, then later he became deaf in one ear. For four of his very last years, he took night classes in oil painting.

When he was 88, he was named the Rutland Senior Citizen of the Year. After he was blind, he learned to weave baskets and donated hundreds to organizations to raise money. He also learned to play the chord organ and made a violin, which he played for various concerts.

He died October 25, 1980, at Rutland, B.C. Although he had to give up woodworking a couple of years before his death, because of his blindness, he continued painting.

YENCHY, VACLA (1844-1921)

Vacla Yechny was born on November 23, 1844. He was a Czech-oslovakian from Bohemia and immigrated from Rytirovelhote (near Prague), possibly about 1893. He took a homestead, but in 1913 when the railway was built and the town site of Esterhazy laid out, he moved there, building a modest residence and attached workshop.

His wife was Frantiska (?-1911), and they had five children. He

Yechny wardrobe

became the organist in the church in Esterhazy and repaired all kinds of musical instruments.

Detail of hand-carving on a wardrobe

He was cabinetmaker, and probably had some training. He brought all his tools, including a foot lathe with him when he immigrated to Canada. He was in demand immediately as a builder for houses and schools. He used fir, maple, birch, and possibly oak and he is most well-known for his furniture such as wardrobes and china cabinets. He also carved crosses for grave markers, built tables, coffins, and a commode (made in 1894, it was once in the Esterhazy Museum).

His work was mostly in the Germanic or Bohemian style. Today a china cabinet is in a private collection, while a wardrobe is in the rectory at the Kaposvar Historical Site near Esterhazy. He died on June 12, 1921, working right up until his death. He's buried in the Esterhazy Cemetery.

ZADEROGNY, (?)
(?-?)

Mr. Zaderogny was born in Ukraine. However, little is known about his early life, not even his first name. It is believed he was an older man when he immigrated to Saskatchewan, perhaps just after the turn of the century. He never took a homestead or had his own place to live. He may have been married, but if so his wife and/or family may have remained in Ukraine.

This cupboard has been stripped of its original paint, but is a fine example of his work.

Above and below: Zaderogny beds. The top one has been stripped except for the uppermost headboard. It was made in 1917

He was, however, an incredible woodworker. Speculation suggests that he must have been trained in some way, because of his expert abilities. He was a carpenter, furniture maker and carver.

It is believed he worked from about 1914 to 1925 in Saskatchewan, but Zaderogny may have arrived, and finished working, much earlier than these dates. He built many buildings, including churches in the Cudworth, Alvena and Prud'homme areas during the summers. In the winter, he resided on various farms where he made elaborate furniture in exchange for his room and board. His furniture was manufactured from heavy planking, perhaps out of fir, but mostly spruce.

He would travel approximately fifty miles to obtain the larger trees or pieces of wood. It is known that he made beds, cupboards, trunks, benches and sleeping benches, and tables, one of which was approximately sixteen feet long. One source suggests that he returned to Ukraine sometime after 1917 (maybe in the 1920s), where he died.

Zaderogny used hand-made tools to make all of his items. Wooden dowels strengthened the pieces. He hand-carved each item elaborately, using his own designs, and then painted them in brilliant colours.

ZAROWNY, PETER
(?-CA. 1966)

Zarowny chair & table

Of Polish descent, Peter Zarowny came from "the old country," (probably Poland, according to distant relatives). He homesteaded at Maloneck in the Arran area on the SW ¼-4-36-31-W1.

He was single, had little family in the area, and never depended on anyone else. His land was left to a distant relative, who eventually lost it to the bank. He died in approximately 1966 in the hospital at Yorkton, and it is believed his is buried in the Benito, Manitoba, town cemetery, as he had lived in the town for the last years of his life.

His work was amateurish and crude, so he probably had little training, although he did have a sense of design. Perhaps only his tools and materials were inferior. He most likely only did work for himself out of necessity, using local materials. He made a chest of drawers, chairs, a washstand, a rocking chair, plain cupboards, and a wood box.

Zarowny washstand

Zarowny cupboard

Ethnic
GROUPS

DOUKHOBOR

S EVERAL COLONIES OF DOUKHOBORS IMMIGRATED TO
Saskatchewan beginning in about 1899. Many of them later moved
to the Castlegar and Grand Forks areas of B.C.

Although they worked communally, many individuals were also
noted. It was part of the doctrine, according to the Doukhobors that "all
men should work in wood." They were continually apprenticing the next
generation of men, passing down their knowledge. They decorated their
furniture with tulips, a traditional design.

Side table (note tulip design)

Popular Doukhobor bed

Doukhobor chair (hand carved)

Doukhobor spindle (Verign Museum)

Doukhobor loom (Verign Museum)

Doukhobor serving spoons

Doukhobor table

Doukhobor frames

Doukhobor "Little People's" cupboard for on a wall

MENNONITES

THE MENNONITES ARE ALSO A GROUP THAT PRODUCED distinctive works of art. They came from Manitoba during a large influx between 1903 and 1906, and settled in the general Swift Current and Rosthern areas. Although they lived in several colonies, they had individual woodworkers, like Mr. Neustaeter and Mr. Schoenfeld, had their own businesses within each community.[1]

Decorative birds

Mennonite cookie cutters

Mennonite dresser

Splint bird (decoration)

Butter press, salad tongs, dough trough, misc. household items

Cradle and stool

Typical Mennonite home with barn attached

Mennonite bench

UKRAINIAN

TRADITIONALLY, UKRAINIANS DIDN'T MAKE CORNER cupboards, although some do exist.² "Ukrainian pieces have little pieces coming off the sides or bases, such as cornices, so the idea of using up what is called "negative spaces" sort of became a way they could express their artistic preference," says Lindsay Anderson, a well known artifact collector from Regina.³

Bench

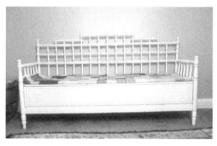

Decorative bird

Candlesticks

Ukrainian cupboard

Ukrainian trunk

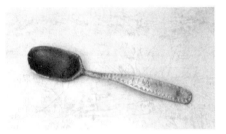

Ukrainian stirring spoon

Cookie cutter

Ukrainian wall shelf

Appendix 1

Locations Of Woodworkers

(Included in this publication)

ANEROID: Nostbakken (Gjert Sr.); Nostbakken (Gjert Nelson Jr.)

ARRAN/PELLY/WHITEBEECH: Zarowny (Peter)

BATOCHE/DUCK LAKE: Dorval (Onésime)

BATTRAM: Levorson (Knut)

BEADLE: Addison (James)

BROADVIEW: Swenson (Nels)

CANORA: Danchilla (John); Samuels (Florian Teodor "Ralph")

CANTEL: Gauthier (Ferdinand)

CODERRE: Smith (Charles)

COXBY: Turner (Philip)

CUDWORTH/ALVENA/WAKAW: Kripki (Sam); Zaderogny (?)

DUBUC: Anderson (Elof John)

DYSART: Roman (Marie)

ESTERHAZY: Yenchy (Vacla)

FLEMING: Vance (Robert)

GLENAVON/BARING: Nelson (Ernest)

GRAVELBOURG: Kliesinger (Joseph)

GRENFELL: Duprau (James Arthur); McJannet (John); Parley (George Elliot & John)

HAFFORD/KRYDOR/ BLAINE LAKE: Hazlebower, (John); Jasieniuk (Joseph); Kadyba (John)

HAZEL DELL: Wilson (Wilfred John)

HUMBOLDT: Novecosky (Jacob)

ITUNA: Dorsch (Joseph)

KENOSEE LAKE: Rogers (Samuel)

KINDERSLEY: Ashley (Arthur)

KIPLING: Abrahamson (Eric); Cunningham (David)

LANGHAM: Berg (Frank)

LAJORD: Hodel (Jacob)

LOON LAKE: Loon Lake Toy Factory (Johan Merz, Franz Rehwald, Heinrich Palme, Anton Hocher, Emil Hecht)

MAPLE CREEK: Hammond (George); Lawrence (William. F)

MAYMONT: Coombs (Harold); Wilmot (Edward)

MEADOW LAKE: Armstrong (Bartley); Caldwell (David)

MELVILLE: Pilon (Joachim)

MOOSOMIN: Charles (Richard Ludlow); McGuirl (John)

NEUDORF: Armbruster (Jacob); Fesser (John); Wendel (Jake)

PERCIVAL: Pearson (Ole Linus)

PIERCELAND: Erikson (Jonas)

PRINCE ALBERT: Nisbet (Rev. James); Pease (George); Russell (Arnold)

PRUD'HOMME: Benoit (Charles Albert); Paquin (Lorenzo)

REGINA: Kleisinger (Joseph)

ROCANVILLE: De Bastien (Rocan)

SOUTHEY: McDonald (Malcom)

TINY: Baker (Niles A.)

WHITEWOOD/NEW FINLAND: Howard (John); Salo (John); Salo (Oscar); Stevens[on] (William ?)

WROXTON: Koshalanych (Alex)

YORKTON: Witow (Frank)

INDIVIDUAL WOODWORKERS

(Included in this publication)

ABRAHAMSON, ERIC (1877-1976): From the Kipling area. Church artifacts.

ADDISON, JAMES (?-1963): Scottish. A carpenter who built a sod house at Beadle (between Kindersley and Netherhill), which has been declared a heritage sight. He also made boxes and furniture for himself.

ANDERSON, ELOF JOHN (1904-1979): Dubuc area. Furniture, toys, skis, buildings, etc.

ARMBRUSTER, JACOB (1854-1935): Neudorf. German. Furniture and tools. Also known as A. J. and "Tischler."

ARMSTRONG, BARTLEY MERETT (1870-1939): Meadow Lake. An ironing board and chair of his are at the Meadow Lake Museum.

ASHLEY, ARTHUR (?-1961): Kindersley area (Beadle) Furniture, coffins, and cabinets.

BENOIT, CHARLES ALBERT (1882-?): Prud'homme. Barns, convent, church steeple and pillars. (Father of Jeanne Sauvé, Governor General of Canada, 1984-89.)

CALDWELL, DAVID (ca. 1871-?): Meadow Lake area. Willow furniture.

CHARLES, RICHARD LUDLOW (?-?): Moosomin. Scottish. Work in the Presbyterian church.

COOMBS, HAROLD JOHN (1885-1964): Maymont. English. Carved figurines, lawn ornaments, knick-knacks from roots, and figures from bits of wood. (Artifacts in Saskatoon.)

CUNNINGHAM, DAVID (?-?): Kipling area. Cabinets, furniture and game tables.

DANCHILLA, JOHN (1903-1979): Canora. Romanian. Furniture and fretwork.

DE BASTIEN, ROCAN (?-?): Rocanville. Made a chair which sits in the Rocanville museum. The town was named after him.

DORSCH, JOSEPH (?-?): Ituna. Corner cupboards and other furniture pieces.

DORVAL, ONÉSIME (1843-1932): Batoche/Duck Lake. Table, wooden flowers and wooden sidewalks. Only woman so far.

DUPRAU, JAMES ARTHUR (1860-1947): Grenfell. A carpenter and woodworker.

ERIKSON, JONAS (?- ?): Pierceland. Miniatures.

FESSER, JOHN (?-ca. 1930s): Neudorf (Abernathy-Lemberg area). German. Cupboards

GAUTHIER, FERDINAND (?-1948): Quebec to Canal. Toys, children's furniture and sculpting.

HAMMOND, GEORGE (1860-1949): Maple Creek area. English. Hand-covered counters and furniture.

HAZLEBOWER, JOHN (?-?): Hafford area. Austrian/German. Prolific builder of small articles for churches.

HODEL, JACOB (1880-1918): Lajord. Carving and picture frames.

HOWARD, JOHN (1877-1966): Whitewood. Violins, bass violins and chairs.

JASIENIUK, JOSEPH (1890-1935): Krydor area. Austrian. Church alters, benches, candle holders, etc.

KADYBA, JOHN (?-ca. 1880s): Hafford area. Polish. Furniture.

KASHTALANYCH, ALEX (?-1937): Wroxton area. Ukrainian. Bench.

KRIPKI, SAM (1883-1970): Cudworth. Ukrainian bread cupboard.

KROCHAK, WILLIAM (1891-1971): Arran/Whitebeech. Church items, furniture, dulcimers, etc.

LAWRENCE, WILLIAM F. (?-?): Maple Creek area. Sash and door company and ran a furniture store.

LEVORSON, KNUT (ca. 1880-1958): Battram. Violins.

LOON LAKE TOY CO-OPERATIVE (ca.1939-1941): Franz Rehwald, Heinrich Palme, Anton Hocher, Emil Hecht and Johan Merz. Loon Lake. Toys.

McDONALD, MALCOLM (1868-1952): Southey. Stone mason, painter, carver, and furniture builder.

MCGUIRL, JOHN (1850-1913): Moosomin area. Scottish. Small furniture factory, ornate desks, tables, and chairs, etc. for Government House, the legislative building, country churches, and masonic lodges.

MCJANNET, JOHN (ca.1862-1911): Grenfell. Carpenter. Cupboards, etc.

NELSON, ERNEST (1876-1940): Glenavon/Baring area. English. Shipbuilder by trade, created furniture, carvings, etc.

NISBET, REV. JAMES (1823-1874): Prince Albert. Furniture.

NOSTBAKKEN, GJERT SR. (1867-1949): Aneroid. Norwegian. Small furniture, built-in cupboards, lathe work, and tools.

NOSTBAKKEN, GJERT NELSON JR. (1894-1975): Aneroid. Norwegian. Small furniture, built-in cupboards, lathe work, and tools.

NOVECOSKY, JACOB (1962-1928): Humboldt. Houses, furniture, wagon wheels, cupboards, picture frames, and coffins.

PAQUIN, LORENZO (1882-1932): Prud'homme. Violins, rocking chairs, and cupboards.

PARLEY, GEORGE ELLIOTT (1870-1949): Grenfell area. Scottish. Structures, furniture, cupboards, hand-carving, and a boat.

PARLEY, JOHN (JACK) (1878-1948): (Brother to George) Grenfell area. Scottish. Structures, furniture, cupboards, and hand-carving.

PEARSON, OLE LINUS (1868-1961): Percival. Scandinavian. Carver and furniture builder.

PEASE, GEORGE (?-?): Prince Albert. Unique chairs.

PERRIN, EDWIN (TED) (1870-1961): Maple Creek area. Store counter.

PILON, JOACHIM (1864-1962): Melville area. Furniture, cabinet maker, and first fire wagon in Melville.

ROGERS, SAMUEL (1872-1961): Kenosee Lake. Buildings, furniture, etc.

ROMAN, MARIE (?-ca 1973): Dysart. Coffins.

RUSSELL, ARNOLD (?-?): Prince Albert area. Small tables.

SALO, JOHN HENRY (1903-1970): (No relation to Oscar Salo.) Whitewood area. Carpenter.

SALO, OSCAR (1873-1966): New Finland (near Tantallon and Whitewood.) Scandinavian. Trinket boxes, wall boxes, interlocking pieces, tables, etc.

SAMUELS, FLORAIN TEODOR (RALPH) (1891-1960): Canora and area. Romanian. Built homes, churches, barns, and furniture.

SMITH, CHARLES (1890-1961): Coderre. English. Furniture out of apple boxes and cheese containers, and fretwork.

STEVENS[ON], WILLIAM? (?-?): Whitewood. English. Carver and furniture maker (bureau's), etc. Hand-carved designs.

SWENSON, NELS (?- ca. 1930s): Broadview. Furniture and carvings.

VANCE, ROBERT (1844-1913): Fleming. Chairs, finishing work and stone masonry.

WENDEL, JACOB (1883-1964): Neudorf. German. Coffins and cupboards.

WILMOT, EDWARD (1880-1963): Maymont area. Carvings in the church.

WILSON, WILFRED JOHN (1882-1980): Hazel Dell. English. Grandfather clocks, etc.

YENCHY, VACLA (1844-1921): Esterhazy area. Czechoslovakian (Bohemian). China cabinets, crosses, coffins, etc.

ZADEROGNY, (?) (?- ca. 1917): Cudworth/Alvena/Meacham. Furniture: beds, tables, etc.

ZAROWNY, PETE (?-ca. 1966): Arran/Pelly. Crude, homemade furniture for his own use.

APPENDIX III

OTHER WOODWORKERS

(These are woodworkers whose names surfaced during the research, but not much information was found on them within the time constraints of the project.)

CERKOWNIAK, ANTHONY: Donated a "holy sepulchre" to the Tiny church in 1933.

DANIELS, FRED: Made rocking chairs and footstools in the Whitewood area.

DEMIC, REV. ?: From Broadview area. He made a pulpit for the Zion Lutheran Church in about 1912 to 1914, and maybe also other items.

GOLD, JOHN LANG: Supposedly made furniture and built houses in Maple Creek.

HARVEY, JOHN: Reputed to have made furniture in the Maple Creek area, which was surely simple in nature, for simple homes, made in a home workshop

KOWALCHUK, ?: He lived in the Ituna area.

LECAIN, ERNIE: A woodworker and blacksmith from the Grenfell area.

LEWIS, C.C.: To Perdue in 1903. Carpenter and furniture maker.

LEWIS, P.H.; To Perdue in 1906. Carpenter and furniture maker.

MARNI, RALPH: Built the St. Joan of Arc Home, and worked at St. Hubert(?). He also painted little pictures for his family. When he made casings to hold windows, he painted little scenes on them.

MARTIN & SONS: Martin & Sons was a cabinet shop in Regina. Mr. Martin also did a lot of the carving on the legislative building. He was raised on a farm in the Fort Qu'Appelle area where he did woodworking in 1926, moving to Regina in 1937.

MacDonald, ?: From Prince Albert. He did a wide variety of work, and hand-carved the pieces. He may be one of the oldest woodworkers.

Miller, Nick: Worked on Zion Lutheran Church at Windthorst.

Moyen, Adelard: A carpenter and furniture builder from St. Denis.

Oakland, Charles: May only be a building contractor from the Broadview area.

Pickering, George: Foam Lake. He did fretwork.

Popov (Popoff), ?: Veregin/Kamsack area. Made chairs, etc.

Sargeant, Rev. J.F.: Made pieces for the St. Luke's Anglican Church in Broadview.

Schmitz, Anton & Clemence: Windthorst. A family of several generations that were wood carvers.

Schmitz, August Mathies: Englefeld.

'76 Ranch: Gull Lake.

Shupe, L. E.: He made a chair using only an axe and a hammer, in the Fort Carlton area.

Silverthorne, Hiram "Hi" (1880-1957): Homesteaded near Kindersly in 1908 on NW 22-30-23-W3 and later farmed N ½-13-30-23-W3. He did woodwork, carvings, etc., including a little stick-man with hinged arms and legs. (No known relationship to the author)

Soehn, Antom: Fox Valley.

Tousignan, ?: Gravelbourg.

Turner, Philip (1839-?): A lay preacher who did much of the carving and woodwork in the church at Coxby. He was born at Cumberland House.

Vaughan, Dorothy: Biggar.

WEINS, AARON: Rapid View. He made willow armchairs, walking canes with carvings, cupboards, and china cabinets.

WILMUT, F. A.: Perdue/Saskatoon. Wood carver and bench carpenter.

WITOW, FRANK: Whitebeech.

WNEK, MIKE: A Polish farmer, who farmed north of Candiac and made picture frames for the Roman Catholic Church and other wood pieces.

WUNSCH, FRED; Leader. Tables, baptismal fonts, etc.

WYATT, SAM: From the Broadview area.

ZEIGLER, MELVIN: Maple Creek. Furniture made with animal horns.

ZUBENKOFF, WASYL: Kamsack/Veregin area. Furniture, frames, and also an instructor.

Appendix iv

Some Types Of Artifacts Made

HOUSEHOLD FURNITURE: tables of varying sizes, chairs, cabinets, china cupboards, dressers, buffets, sideboards, wardrobes, stools, footstools, beds, benches, settees, spice racks, breadboxes, hanging wall cupboards, rocking chairs, shelves, trunks, cradles, cribs, bookcases, washstands, chests, desks, couches, grandfather clocks.

HOUSEHOLD NECESSITIES AND ODDITIES: dough troughs, ironing boards, toiletry racks, rolling pins, lamps, bowls, containers, spoons, butter churns, flour grinders, candle holders, cookie cutters, coffee containers, spinning wheels, looms, sewing boxes, handkerchief boxes, trinket boxes, ornaments, birchbark and carved flowers, splint birds, knick-knacks, plant stands, picture frames.

MASONIC LODGE FURNITURE: chairs, podiums, tables, columns.

LEGISLATIVE FURNITURE: speaker's chairs, desks.

TOYS, GAMES, FIGURINES: pull-toys, sleds, toboggans, skis, tricycles, rocking horses, wagons, dolls, board games, figurines, animals, birds, miniatures and replicas.

MUSICAL INSTRUMENTS: violins, dulcimers, cellos.

TOOLS: lathes, wood planes, saws, chisels, knives, rope makers, tool boxes, clamps.

RELIGIOUS ARTIFACTS: candleholders, icons, Eucharist churches, crosses, grave markers, pulpits, altars, bishop chairs, pews, bible holders, hymn boards, wall plaques, figurines, communion tables, coffins, Jewish carrying tables, prayer tables.

MISCELLANEOUS: whirligigs, fire wagons, doghouses, plank sidewalks, yard ornaments, boats, hockey sticks, cameras.

BIBLIOGRAPHY

Bird, Michael & Kobayaski, Terry. *A Splendid Harvest: Germanic Folk & Decorative Arts in Canada*. Toronto: Van Nostrant Reinhold Ltd, 1981. (library call no 745-0971B)

Blanchette, Jean-Francois and others. *From the Heart, Folk Art in Canada*. Toronto: McLelland and Stewart in co-operation with the National Museum of Man, National Museums of Canada, 1983. (library call # 745.0971)

Burnham, Dorothy K. *Unlike the Lilies: Dukhobour Textile Traditions in Canada*. Toronto: Royal Ontario Museum, 1986. (library call no. 74600899B)

The Canadian Collector, 1973, July/August. An article on collections in the west.

Centennial Tribute: Oakshella, Broadview, Percival 1882-1982/spine title: *Story of Broadview and area, 1982*. Published by the Broadview Pioneer History Society.

Echoes From the Past: St. Matthew's Forest Farm, 1895-1980. Edited by Jesse & Sylvia Howard.

Hall, Trevor. *Royal Canada*. Goldaming, Surrey, England: Archive Publishing, a subsidiary of Colour Library Books Ltd, 1989.

La Patriote de l'Ouest 14-12-32:1 (re Dorval).

Moosomin History Society. *Moosomin—One Century—Town and Country*.

Nancy Mattson Schelstraete (editor). New Finland Historical and Heritage Society. *Life in the New Finland Woods: A History of New Finland, Saskatchewan.* Edmonton Alberta: Ronald's Western Printing, 1982.

Plath, Iona. *The Decorative Arts of Sweden.* New York: Charles Scribner's Sons Ltd, 1948.

Polachic, Darlene. "The Prince Who Became Rancher," *Western Producer Magazine,* Western People section, May 13, 1993, p.1.

Refsal, Harley. *Woodcarving in the Scandinavian Style.* New York: Sterling Publishing Co. Inc., 1992, p. 15-18.

Saskatchewan Culture and Youth Cultural Activities Branch—arts section. *Saskatchewan Craftspeople.* Saskatoon: Modern Press, 1979. (library call # 745.097124)

Gordon Barnhart. *Sentinel of the Prairies: the Saskatchewan Legislative Building* Has photos of old legislative building on Dewdney Ave, plus speaker's chairs and other furniture.

The Illustrated Encyclopedia of Woodworking Handtools.

ABOUT THE AUTHOR

Judith Silverthorne is the author of three other books, a biography called *Made in Saskatchewan: Peter Rupchan, Ukrainian Pioneer and Potter,* and two children's novels: *The Secret of Sentinel Rock,* for which she won the 1996 Saskatchewan Book Award for Children's Literature, and *Dinosaur Hideout,* which has been nominated for the same award in 2003. Her work has also appeared in many periodicals and anthologies.

During the last few years she has also worked as an editor, curator, and a television documentary producer, operating her own production and publishing company, Spiral Communications Inc., as well as working as the Executive Director for the Saskatchewan Library Association. Silverthorne has lived most of her life in Saskatchewan, and is keenly interested in history of the province, which inspires many of her works. She currently lives in Regina with her teenage son and is at work on sequels of her children's novels, as well as an adult mystery novel.

A selection of woodworkers from I*ngrained Legacy: Saskatchewan Pioneer Woodworkers 1870-1930* were profiled in a television documentary and series of vignettes, both of which are available for purchase through the author.

If you enjoyed this book by Judith Silverthorne, you may also enjoy...

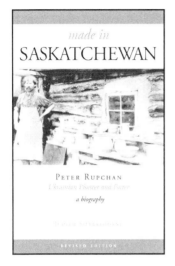

MADE IN SASKATCHEWAN:

Peter Rupchan, Ukrainian Pioneer & Potter. A biography

Peter Rupchan was more than just another Ukrainian pioneer trying to survive the hardships and personal tragedies of early settlement on the prairies. He was innovative, eccentric and industrious. When he immigrated to Saskatchewan in 1905, he was also determined to establish a viable pottery industry.

Although he became one of the earliest potters in the province, and the only one to travel extensively with his wares, his life was a constant struggle. Through the bleakest of times, he was faced with numerous tragedies and disasters that plagued him until his untimely death in 1944. Somehow he persevered while managing to find local clay on his farm, capturing the wind to grind his clay and glazes, and utilizing a variety of other natural means to produce what are today considered valuable works of art.

This revised edition contains all the riveting text of the original book, with added notations and extra photographs of Rupchan's work.

108 PAGES • SOFTCOVER • 6" X 9" • ISBN: 0-21435-04-5 • $13.50 CDN

CONTENTS

DIFFERENT KINDS OF HOCKEY

Hockey is a popular sport played by people all over the world. There are many different versions, or kinds, of hockey. It's easy to figure out where ice hockey is played—on ice! Another kind of hockey is field hockey.

Field hockey is a game played with a stick and a ball. It's most often played on grass or man-made **turf**. In the United States, field hockey is played mainly by girls and women in high school and college. Playing field hockey is a great way to learn skills such as teamwork while having fun outside with your friends!

Overtime!

While field hockey is mainly a women's sport in the United States, it's played by both men and women in equal numbers in other parts of the world.

Girls Play

Girls
JOIN THE
TEAM

FIELD HOCKEY

David Anthony

PowerKiDS
press.

New York

Published in 2017 by The Rosen Publishing Group, Inc.
29 East 21st Street, New York, NY 10010

First Edition

Editor: Katie Kawa
Book Design: Tanya Dellaccio

Photo Credits: Cover Aspen Photo/Shutterstock.com; pp. 5, 22 Air Images/ Shutterstock.com; p. 7 (bottom) https://commons.wikimedia.org/wiki/File:Relief_ pentelic_marble_%22Ball_Players%22_510-500_BC,_NAMA_3476_102587.jpg; p. 7 (top) https://commons.wikimedia.org/wiki/File:Constance_Applebee_ circa_1903.jpg; p. 10 Kansas City Star/Getty Images; p. 11 Corepics VOF/ Shutterstock.com; p. 13 Boston Globe/Getty Images; p. 15 (both) Brian A. Westerholt/ Getty Images; p. 17 Pascal Le Segretain/Getty Images; p. 19 (top) Daniel Garcia/ Getty Images; p. 19 (bottom) LatinContent/STR/Getty Images; p. 21 (top) Al Bello/ Getty Images; p. 21 (bottom) B Bennett/Getty Images.

Cataloging-in-Publication Data

Names: Anthony, David.
Title: Girls play field hockey / David Anthony.
Description: New York : PowerKids Press, 2017. | Series: Girls join the team | Includes index.
Identifiers: ISBN 9781499420975 (pbk.) | ISBN 9781499420999 (library bound) | ISBN 9781499420982 (6 pack)
Subjects: LCSH: Field hockey–Juvenile literature.
Classification: LCC GV1017.H7 A548 2017 | DDC 796.355–d23

Manufactured in the United States of America

CPSIA Compliance Information: Batch #BS16PK For Further Information contact Rosen Publishing, New York, New York at 1-800-237-9932

Field hockey is just called "hockey" in most countries. However, its full name is most often used in the United States and Canada because of the popularity of ice hockey in those countries.

AN ANCIENT SPORT

Field hockey has been around for thousands of years! It's believed people in ancient Egypt might have played a kind of field hockey. Other versions were played by the ancient Romans and the ancient Aztec people who lived in what's now Mexico. In the mid-1800s, field hockey became very popular in England. The Hockey Association in London was founded in 1886, and this group made a set of basic rules for the sport.

Until the late 1800s, only men were allowed to play field hockey. The first women's field hockey club was founded in 1887. After that, women's field hockey began to grow in popularity.

Overtime!

In 1927, the International Federation of Women's Hockey Associations was created. This organization helped field hockey become a sport played by women around the world.

Constance Applebee introduced field hockey to women in the United States in 1901. While studying in the United States, Constance, who grew up in England, showed women at Harvard University how to play the sport. After that, field hockey was played by women at other U.S. colleges.

Constance Applebee

stone carving of field hockey from ancient Greece

7

THE RULES OF THE GAME

Field hockey players score points by shooting the ball into the other team's goal using their stick. Each goal in field hockey is worth one point. Goals can only be scored from inside the part of the field called the shooting circle or striking circle. If a shot is taken from outside the circle, the ball must touch another player in the circle before going in the goal to score a point.

Field hockey players can't use their feet to score or to move the ball down the field. Using small taps of the stick to move the ball down the field is called dribbling.

Overtime!

Field hockey games are also called matches. A field hockey match is most often broken into two halves that are each 35 minutes long.

The field where field hockey is played is
90 yards (91.4 m) long and 60 yards (54.9
m) wide. Players have to be in good shape to run
and down such a long field!

□ goal   □ shooting circle

EACH PLAYER'S JOB

Each field hockey team must have 11 players on the field at one time. Teams are made up of offensive players, midfielders, defensive players, and a goalkeeper. Offensive players are called forwards, and defensive players are also known as fullbacks.

A forward's job is to score goals, while a fullback's job is to stop the other team's forwards from scoring. A midfielder plays both offense and defense. This means she helps her team score and helps stop the other team from scoring. A goalkeeper's job is to stop the ball from going in the goal. She gets to use her feet and other body parts that the rest of the players can't use.

goalkeeper

Field hockey players can pass the ball to each other by pushing it with their stick. Fullbacks try to break up these passes to give their team the ball.

Overtime!

Midfielders must be able to run all over the field to play both offense and defense. They run more than any other kind of field hockey player.

GEAR FOR THE GAME

If you want to play field hockey, all you really need is a ball and a stick. A field hockey stick is shaped like the letter "J," and it has a rounded side and a flat side. Players use the flat side to move the ball.

Although the ball used to play field hockey is small, it can be hit at the goal with enough power to hurt a goalkeeper. That's why goalkeepers wear special safety **equipment**. This gear includes a helmet, a chest **protector**, and pads for different parts of their arms and legs.

Overtime!

A field hockey ball can be shot with so much power that it travels up to 100 miles (161 km) per hour!

goggles

★ protect the eyes

mouth guard

★ protects the teeth and the rest of the mouth

FIELD HOCKEY SAFETY EQUIPMENT

shin guards

★ protect the lower legs and ankles and are often worn with high socks over them

shoes (cleats)

★ help players run safely on the field

These are the basic pieces of safety equipment worn by field hockey players. Some defensive players also wear masks to protect their face at certain times.

COLLEGE AND BEYOND

If you work hard on the field and in the classroom, you could play field hockey in college. The **National Collegiate Athletic Association** (NCAA) holds a tournament, or set of games, every year to **determine** the best college field hockey team in the United States.

The best field hockey players in the world face each other every four years in the Hockey World Cup. The first Women's World Cup was played in 1974. While the United States takes part in the Women's World Cup, it's never won this tournament. As of 2014, the only countries that have won the Women's World Cup are Germany, Australia, Argentina, and the Netherlands.

Overtime!

The NCAA field hockey tournament began in 1981, and it's only for women's teams. There's no men's NCAA field hockey tournament.

Old Dominion University holds the record for the most NCAA field hockey **championships**. As of 2015, this school has won nine championships. The University of Maryland's field hockey team, shown here, is a close second with eight championships.

AT THE OLYMPICS

Field hockey is a popular sport at the Summer Olympics, which are also held every four years. Like the World Cup, the Olympics feature the world's best field hockey players. The first time field hockey was introduced as an Olympic sport was 1908, but that was only men's field hockey.

Women's field hockey became part of the Olympics in 1980. The U.S. women's field hockey team won a bronze **medal** at the 1984 Olympics, which were held in Los Angeles, California. USA Field Hockey runs camps and other programs you can take part in if you want to play in the Olympics one day!

Overtime!

In 2014, the 1984 Olympic field hockey team was **inducted** into the USA Field Hockey Hall of Fame.

Kate Middleton

During the 2012 Summer Olympics in London, England, Kate Middleton, the Duchess of Cambridge, was often seen supporting the British women's field hockey team. Kate played field hockey while she was in school before becoming a member of the British royal family.

"THE MAGICIAN"

Luciana Aymar is considered one of the best female field hockey players of all time. She was born in Argentina, and she became the youngest member ever of that country's national field hockey team. Luciana won four Olympic medals, and she also won four Hockey World Cup medals. She's the only player to win the International Hockey Federation Player of the Year **award** eight times.

In 2015, Luciana was chosen to be an **ambassador** for the 2018 Youth Olympic Games in Argentina. She wants to grow the sport in her home country by helping young people learn to play field hockey.

Overtime!

Luciana Aymar stopped playing for Argentina's national field hockey team in 2014. She scored 162 goals while playing for her country.

Luciana Aymar

Luciana Aymar was so good at field hockey that her nickname was "The Magician."

INDOORS AND ON ICE

Field hockey can also be played inside. Indoor field hockey, or indoor hockey, is very similar to outdoor field hockey, but it's played by teams of six on an indoor field. A U.S. national team plays indoor field hockey matches around the world.

If these versions of hockey sound fun to you, ice hockey might also be a sport you'd like to play. Like indoor field hockey, ice hockey features teams of six players. These players try to get a puck into the other team's goal while skating on ice. This sport is growing in the United States, and many communities have ice hockey teams for girls.

Overtime!

The National Women's Hockey **League** is a **professional** ice hockey league for women in the United States. It started in 2015.

Women's ice hockey became an Olympic sport in 1998. That year, the United States took home the gold medal. Since then, the U.S. team has won three silver medals and one bronze medal.

LEARNING ON THE FIELD

You can play hockey inside or outside, on ice or on an outdoor field. No matter where you play it, this sport teaches the value of hard work and **cooperation**. It also teaches you how much fun it is to get moving and be active.

Field hockey is the most popular version of hockey played around the world. It's been around for centuries in different forms, and women have been playing this sport for more than 100 years. Today, girls and women still enjoy playing field hockey—whether it's on a school field or Olympic turf!

GLOSSARY

ambassador: An official messenger or representative.

award: A prize given for doing something well.

championship: A contest to find out who's the best player or team in a sport.

cooperation: The act of working with others to get something done.

determine: To officially decide something.

equipment: Supplies or tools needed for a certain purpose.

induct: To officially make a person a member of a group or organization.

league: A group of teams that play the same sport and compete against each other.

medal: A flat, small piece of metal with art or words that's used as an honor or reward.

National Collegiate Athletic Association: The organization that governs college sports in the United States.

professional: Having to do with a job someone does for a living.

protector: Something that keeps someone or something safe.

turf: The upper layer of soil that is a thick mat of grass and plant roots.

WEBSITES

Due to the changing nature of Internet links, PowerKids Press has developed
an online list of websites related to the subject of this book. This site is
updated regularly. Please use this link to access the list:
www.powerkidslinks.com/gjt/fhoc